A Guide to NEW HALL
Porcelain Patterns

A Guide to NEW HALL
Porcelain Patterns

A. de Saye Hutton

BARRIE & JENKINS
LONDON

First published in Great Britain in 1990 by
Barrie & Jenkins Ltd
20 Vauxhall Bridge Road
London SW1V 2SA

British Library Cataloguing in Publication Data
De Saye Hutton, Anthony
   A guide to New Hall porcelain patterns.
   1. New Hall porcelain — Collectors' guides
   I. Title
   738.2'7

   ISBN 0 7126 3579 3

Typeset by SX Composing Ltd, Rayleigh, Essex
Printed and bound in England by Butler & Tanner,
Frome, Somerset
Designed by Carol McCleeve

Contents

*Dedicated to my wife Ann
without whose knowledgeable
assistance, advice, and
encouragement this book would
not have been written.*

Foreword

THE MOST FREQUENTLY POSED QUESTION *to me regarding possible reference books is 'Can you publish a book on pattern numbers?' This new work at once illustrates the great difficulties and the real benefits!*

Anthony and Ann de Saye Hutton have been collecting New Hall porcelains for over twenty-five years, paying particular attention to the patterns and their numbers. They have visited a vast number of collections both private and public, and numerous collectors have kindly kept them informed as new designs are discovered. In recent years this research has been made a little less difficult as the material has been stored on a computer.

Here then is twenty-five or more years' extensive research: yet the authors are still only able to record a quite small proportion of the three thousand or so designs which this important porcelain manufactory produced (through various partnerships) from the early 1780s into the early or mid 1830s. To be meaningful all, or most, of the identified designs have to be illustrated or very fully described. Mere numbers are certainly not enough, as every factory would have, for example, a pattern 100 or 200. It is only relevant and helpful when one can see what design should bear that (or any other) number. Conversely, a pattern is not helpful without its number for in many cases the New Hall Company copied another firm's design, or their own was copied by other manufacturers. One must have a design and its correct number. Those are a few of the difficulties of listing the ceramic design of any one firm when, as in this case, the original records have been lost.

The benefits of such (even incomplete) research is self-evident, especially when so few pieces bear a factory mark. All collectors of New Hall porcelain or of late eighteenth and early nineteenth-century porcelain in general owe the de Saye Huttons and their publishers a great debt. For this, I believe, is the first experiment in publishing, in hardback form, a record of a factory's designs. May many more follow this lead.

7

Preface

DURING TWENTY-FIVE YEARS OF collecting and/or recording patterns
I have, with the invaluable help of fellow collectors and dealers, built up a
sufficiently large reference file of photographs, drawings and descriptions to
enable me to reconstruct at least part of a pattern book. Over the years many
people have asked me to publish the results of my researches and I now feel
that it is time I committed them to paper.

The point of this work is not to supersede the other excellent publications
on this subject (see Bibliography) but to supplement them and be of assistance
in the attribution of patterns. I also hope that readers will be able to confirm
doubtful numbers, add new patterns, and ascribe numbers to the chapter
Patterns without Numbers.

A Brief History of New Hall

NEW HALL (HEATH, WARBURTON & CO.) started in 1781 with the manufacture of hard-paste porcelain when the founders, John Turner, Anthony Keeling, Jacob Warburton, Samuel Hollins, Charles Bagnall, Joshua Heath, William Clewes, and John Hollins acquired the patent from Champion of Bristol. John Turner and Anthony Keeling left the partnership in 1782 and John Daniel joined as manager. At this time the company was known as Hollins, Warburton & Co. (Later Hollins, Warburton, Daniel & Co.) The only other names connected with the factory are Peter Warburton, who invented the process for printing scenes in gold, and Fidelle Duvivier the distinguished painter and decorator.

The hard-paste period ended with pattern numbers in the low 1000s with pattern no. 1046 being the highest so far recorded.

In about 1812 the company changed to the manufacture of bone china, at which time the New Hall concentric ring mark was introduced. It must be remembered that early patterns and their numbers were sometimes reused on bone china whilst at other times new numbers were allocated to the pattern (e.g. 709 and 1063).

The use of the concentric ring mark seems to have been discontinued well before the works closed in 1835. (Pattern no. 1830 is the highest I have come across with this mark.) Round about pattern no. 2000 production seems to have fallen into two very different categories: one is rather crude in the potting and simple or naive in decoration, the other is finely potted and extremely sophisticated in decoration. The difference is so marked that they could be of different manufacture.

In 1831 the factory was unsuccessfully put up for auction and was later rented out. The final closure and sale of stock did not take place until 1835.

For more detailed information on the history of the factory the reader is directed to various other publications mentioned in the Bibliography.

List of Colour Plates

A Pattern 761 Teapot: height 15.5cm

B Pattern 425 Clip-handled Jug: height 19cm

C Pattern 421 Coffee-pot and Stand: height 27cm

D Pattern 241 Clip-handled Jug: height 15cm

E A selection of Barrel-shaped Teapots: top left pattern 121, right pattern 20, bottom left pattern 122, centre ref. U186, right pattern 139

F A selection of Silver-shaped Teapots: top left pattern 171, right pattern 78, bottom left pattern 136, right pattern 273

G A selection of Ogee-oval-shaped Teapots: top pattern 208, bottom left pattern 449, right pattern 241

H A selection of Boat-shaped Teapots: top left pattern 781, right pattern 829, bottom left pattern 554, right ref. U50 marked 'Cotton High Street Edinburgh'

I A selection of London-shaped Teapots: top left pattern 1614, right pattern 1695, bottom left pattern 1163, right pattern 1453

J A selection of Sucriers: top left pattern 202, centre ref. U30, right pattern 319, bottom left pattern 490, centre pattern 155, right pattern 427

K A selection of Sucriers: top left pattern 408, right pattern 636, bottom left pattern 306, centre pattern 213, right pattern 446

L A selection of Helmet-shaped Jugs: top left pattern 89, centre pattern 140, right pattern 144, bottom left to right pattern 53, pattern 155, pattern 173, ref. U81

M A selection of Jugs: top left pattern 83, centre ref. U27, right pattern 172, bottom left pattern 191, centre ref. U185, right pattern 243

N A selection of Jugs: top left pattern 22, centre pattern 273, right ref. U148, bottom left pattern 222, centre pattern 296, right pattern 449

O A late Sucrier of rare shape, pattern 2901: height 14.5cm

P A pair of well decorated dessert Plates, pattern 2932: size 24.5cm

Acknowledgements

This work would have been impossible without the invaluable help of the many collectors, dealers and museum curators who have supplied me with information, photographs and drawings or have allowed me to examine and photograph pieces from their collections. A list of these contributors is included below and I sincerely hope that anyone who has inadvertently been omitted will accept my apologies.

Mrs M. W. Andrews, Dr and Mrs Geoffrey M. Barnes, Mr Donald Beaton, Susan Beaumont, Derek H. Chitty, Coombe Valley Antiques, Mr and Mrs C. F. Critchley, J. Dermody, R. C. F. Dibben, Richard Earle, Geoffrey A. Godden, Mrs N. Gunson, Mrs A. R. Hobbs, D. Holgate, M. Holliday, Dr M. S. Johnson, Messrs Klaber & Klaber, N. Lazarus, Dr J. McCarthy, Mrs C. I. McIntyre, Mrs J. V. McNeile, Philip Miller, Mr and Mrs L. P. R. Pailthorpe, Mrs K. Paisley, Mr and Mrs M. Preller, Mrs J. B. Reed, Maj. M. C. Smith, P. A. Stevenson, City Museum and Art Gallery Stoke-on-Trent, Lady Thomas, Sally Turner, Messrs Vincent Thomas Antiques, D. G. Warner, Whittington Antiques, Mrs E. Wilderspin, Mrs A. Wildish.

The following illustrations are from the Godden Collection: Plates 1, 10, 34, 115, 196, 198, 205, 209, 213, 218, 220, 224, 227, 231, 232, 233, 271, 290, 294, 307.

Introduction

A S FAR AS IS KNOWN THERE is no New Hall pattern book in existence and to date only about 400 different patterns have been described or illustrated in books and other publications. Assuming there were no gaps in the consecutive numbering, it would seem that there could be in excess of 3500 patterns or variations. Some patterns either have never been marked or have not been allocated numbers. (Very early patterns, silver lustre and blue and white, unless gilded, seem to come into this category.)

Most people think of New Hall as being producers of spriggy, cottage-type tea and coffee wares. However this is far from the case, as there are many examples of dessert services, some breakfast sets, and even asparagus servers, flasks, and cutlery. A very high proportion of the decoration was extremely sophisticated and heavily gilded.

The majority of the patterns described have been fairly well substantiated, but there is always some doubt where only one marked piece has been seen as there is a small but significant number of errors in pattern·number marking. There are a few examples of identical or near identical decoration appearing under two or more differing numbers (e.g. 1453, 1485, 1830). In some cases these may be caused by transposition of digits. Verification of attribution of the pattern numbers above 2500 is made very difficult because so few examples have been found and there is therefore a lack of continuity and progressive trend.

In order to make the list of patterns as comprehensive as possible, I have included these late patterns attributed to, and now generally accepted as being, New Hall plus a few rather vague descriptions based on information which has not been fully verified.

It can be generally accepted that, apart from a very few examples in the very late bone period, New Hall did not mark cups, saucers, tea bowls, and cans with pattern numbers. Out of the thousands of these items that I must have seen I only know of two cases in the earlier period and can only conclude that they were either marked in error or were replacements. I am of the opinion that pieces marked with a pattern number should be rejected as New Hall unless there is either strong confirmatory evidence or they are of the very late bone period.

In addition to the Ring Mark and workmens' marks, other marks attributed to or found on New Hall pieces are the still controversial Frankenthal Lion which appears only on some early blue and white patterns, including tea bowls, a Crown with Warburtons Patent on gold prints, and two retailers' marks, Abbott and Mist, Fleet Street and Cotton, High Street, Edinburgh. Pieces with this last mark seem to date from *c.*1806-*c.*1809 at which time Elijah

Cotton had his glass, china, and stone warehouse in the High Street. In 1810 he moved to 43, Hanover Street and continued trading there until 1831. He may have continued using his old mark during some of this period but this would seem to be unlikely as so far no piece of bone china has turned up bearing this inscription. Recently a very rare relief-moulded pad-mark with the initials NH, found on a few bone china jugs or mugs with applied floral decoration, has been attributed to New Hall.

Patterns with Known Numbers

THE NUMBER AT THE TOP LEFT hand corner of each item is the pattern number, an R immediately following this denotes that a New Hall concentric ring mark has been seen on an item decorated with this pattern. Any subsequent number or numbers on the same line are of similar or associated patterns; a U preceding a number denotes a reference to the serial number of an item in the next chapter, Patterns without Numbers. In certain circumstances this space may have been used for remarks.

In the main description of a pattern a 'coloured edge' means that the edge line overlaps or at least reaches the edge of the item. A 'border line' or 'border lines' can mean either an isolated line or lines between the edges of an item or the outlining of another colour or part of a pattern. In the main this type of description applies to gilded patterns.

3 Border of two narrow magenta bands separated by small circles with blue dot. Main spray consists of a mauve flower, a magenta flower, small mauve flowers, small blue flowers, and green foliage.

5 Mazarine blue border overgilded with leaves in arrowhead formation. Central Duvivier painted polychrome rural scene of bird on foliage-covered tree stump with lake, island, and boat in background.

11 Scalloped gold edge line. Duvivier decorated polychrome scene of exotic birds.

12 Pink band border overlaid with simple line design in a darker pink with interconnected loops below. Three small sprays of flowers also in two-tone pink.

13 Gold rim and single gold leafy sprig. See p. 80.

20 Magenta edge and border of a straight line and an arched line separated by four blue dots. Oriental scene of a figure with a parasol and another with a toy windmill and a flower. Magenta, blue, green, and yellow. Pl. 1 and Col. Pl. E.

22 Blue edge. A band of criss-cross magenta lines and dots with blue semicircles under. Main spray has large magenta flower, yellow flower with iron-red stamens, a small blue flower, green leaves. Col. Pl. N.

52 Gold edge. Undulating gold line over a plain gold band with gold dots and gold star devices on short stalks. Pl. 2. See p. 80.

53 189 Overall decoration of sprigs with single magenta flower and gold leaves. Wavy-edged gold band border. Col. Pl. L.

62 98 Gold edge and border line, the inner border of two-tone gold husks is crossed by a wavy gold line. See p. 80.

64 138, 175, 176, 283 Gold edge and border bands. See p. 80.

67 Pink scale band with iron-red edge and mauve swags below. Polychrome sprigs at junctions.

78 Pink scale border band broken by mauve ( ) shaped devices. Beneath are simply-decorated swags with pink roses and green leaves at junctions. Col. Pl. F.

81 Gold edge. Border decoration: gold line with periodic groups of arrow heads and either side gold shallow inverted swags with trefoils at junctions. See p. 80.

83 Gold edge and border lines with border of gold triangular devices containing a pink rose with green leaves. From each is suspended five gold pendants. Col. Pl. M.

84 U25 Gold edge. Green border line with leaf sprays attached on alternate sides and a wavy gold line with single gold flowers and stalks attached entwined about it. Pl. 3.

89 444 Gold edge and border lines. A border of large gold ovals each containing a magenta dash and joined by connected pairs of magenta trefoil devices. Col. Pl. L.

90 136 Gold edge. Gold wavy-line border with spaced along it a six-dot magenta flower with three black leaves either side. Central motif echoes flowers.

91 Gold edge. Wavy line, straight line, and line of inverted swags with grenades at junctions and inter-spersed dots all in gold. See p. 80.

94 Gold edge. Two black lines with magenta arrowhead swags between and gold pendants at junctions. Inner gold line with one serrated edge. Pl. 4.

98 62 Brown edge. A border of two-tone green husks separated by orange dots is crossed by an undulating line of blue dots.

101 (Not confirmed.) Iron-red border with mauve edges. Mauve swags with single pink rose at bottom and small mauve flowers and green foliage either side. Odd sprigs. Pl. 5.

115 Border: single gold line with two crossing wavy gold lines beneath, a mid blue horizontal dash is within the oval formed by these lines. See p. 80.

121 Iron-red edge and border lines. Iron-red bells have polychrome floral sprays hanging from them and are connected by a mauve line with feathers at ends and a small centre sprig. Other leaf sprigs. Col. Pl. E.

122 Magenta edge. Border of ma-genta hearts between two lines under which are a straight and an arched black line with blue dots. Centre line of magenta hearts crossed by un-dulating green foliage. Col. Pl. E.

124 (Not confirmed.) Gold edge. Gold-edged broad orange inner border with sets of three angled gold lines running to edge forming frames containing four small circles each with a dot and a six-petal gold flowerlet.

130 Gold edge and border line. Decoration is comprised of sprays of single-stalk gold flowers with drooping heads. (Also unconfirmed report of a puce version.) See p. 80.

133 All black decoration. Border line with attached loops under and beneath which is a line of dots. Floral spray of which three roses are the main items.

135 Gold edge and inner gold band between which are ovals containing starbursts with orange centres joined by wavy foliage all in gold with single orange flowerlets. Pl. 6.

136 90 Gold edge and border line. An undulating gold line of spaced six-petal flowers with orange centres and two gold leaves, a further leaf on the gold line separates the flowers. Col. Pl. F.

138 64, 175, 176, 283 Plain gold edge. Pl. 7.

139 Magenta edge and border lines. An iron-red border line beneath which are mauve leafy swags with single red daisy joined by straight line and half daisy. Main polychrome spray with magenta rose. Col. Pl. E.

140 605 Magenta edge line. Pale magenta border band painted with darker edges, loops, and dots with green zigzag line below. Main spray in iron-red, mauve, and green features a large magenta rose. Col. Pl. L.

141 A broken border of three blue lines with criss-cross dark orange lines and dots between. Main floral decoration in blue and orange has blue-framed rural scene in orange and some blue superimposed.

142 148, U44 Gold edge and border lines. An undulating line of fawn feathers is crossed by an undulating line of gold dots with a larger dot at each intersection. (Also with gold stars and dots border added.) Pl. 8.

144 Magenta border line. A border band of mauve dots between iron-red lines above an undulating foliate line in green, mauve, and magenta. Main spray features four roses in mauve and magenta. Col. Pl. L.

145 245 All gold swags with dark blue enamel border line. Pl. 9.

148 142, U44 Gold edge and border lines. Undulating lines of orange feathers and gold dots crossing. Large gold dot at intersection. Border broken at intervals by gold garland with central gold star. Pl. 10.

149 ?240 and 249 are identical. Gold edges and border lines. Narrow mazarine blue band overgilt with arrows and dots with below a further arched mazarine blue border with gold triangles, rising sun motifs and long pendants from points. Pl. 11.

150 (Not confirmed.) Gold border band with bows and leaves under. Gold-edged mazarine blue band overdecorated with line of gold blobs.

152 Gold edge. Wave-shaped mazarine blue border with foliate overgilding and gold swags from wave tips. Inner border of gold line crossed by undulating gold foliate line.

153 Gold edge and border lines. Mazarine blue border arched on lower side decorated with gold stars and dots. Beneath are gold swags alternately of dots and crosses with pendants at alternate junctions. Pl. 12.

154 Gold edge and border lines between which is a zigzag mazarine blue device with single gold stars between.

155 Gold edge and border lines. Mazarine blue band looped on lower side and overgilt with loops and dots. Inner border of a gold line with an arched line under and gold trefoils at junctions. Col. Pls J and L.

156 Gold edge. Wavy mazarine blue line of regular varying width and with gold edges crossed by a wavy dotted gold line. There are single gold stars between and gold slashes outside. Pl. 13.

157 Iron-red line and looped line border. Polychrome oriental scene of three figures, one with parasol and one with mandolin, at a table with flower vase. Colours: blue, magenta, iron-red, green.

160 Gold edge. Complex, slightly scrolled, gold decoration forms six (on saucer) cartouches, in each of which is a swag of three pink roses and green foliage. Pl. 14.

161 Gold edge and border line between which is a blue and gold foliate band. Overall blue and gold sprigs. Pl. 15.

166 Gold edge and border line. Large gold floral swags with short pendants at joins. Emerald green and orange floral devices within the swags.

167 206, 221, 222, 254, 257, 258 Gold edge and border lines. Medium size peach band between gold lines. Gold sprigs.

168 Gold edge and border bands. Medium-size peach band with same colour rose and foliate swags below. Gold dots at joins.

170 U81, U112, U272 Gold edges and border lines. A border of mazarine blue scrolls, gold edged. The connecting ovals are overgilt with a ring of dots and a large centre dot. All entwined by wavy line of gold foliage.

171 U57 (also in black) Borders of mauve dots between two iron-red lines and an undulating line edged with dots. Main motif is a shallow iron-red basket filled with floral spray. Col. Pl. F.

172 Magenta edge. An undulating mauve ribbon is crossed by a straight magenta line. Small polychrome floral sprays above the ribbon and on the main body. Col. Pl. M.

173 The pink scale border has occasional scrolls beneath from which hang coloured floral sprays. There is an undulating brown line edged with dots. Small coloured sprays on main body. Col. Pl. L.

175 64, 138, 176, 283 Single gold line near edge. Main decoration is of a few sprays of gold foliage. See p. 80.

176 64, 138, 175, 283 Gold edge with gold inner line between which are a few sprays of gold foliage.

180 Gold edge and gold base line with a sparse sprinkling of gold stars overall. See p. 80.

181 Gold edge and border lines. Pale green band is decorated with white and gold ovals and dots. Beneath are gold swags and a line of evenly-spaced gold sprigs.

182 Gold edge and border line. Inner border of large turquoise dots. An undulating gold ribbon is crossed by an undulating gold line of foliage with single flower. All-over gold sprigs. Pl. 16.

183 Gold edge and border lines between which is a band of mauve dotted ovals with green centres broken by oval cartouches with pink roses. Lower band has curved fronds under. Gold stars on main body.

185 Gold edge, gold line inner border with gold diamond shapes with pendants joined by leafy swags with interspersed pink roses which have pendant green foliage. Pl. 17.

186 Undulating magenta ribbon with floral sprigs within the loops. A green foliate line entwined about two fine iron-red lines. Small polychrome sprigs on body.

188 Gold edge. Two inner gold lines between which is a dotted gold wavy line crossed by a green wavy foliage line with pairs of orange hips.

189 53 Gold edge and border lines. Scattered orange and gold floral sprigs. Pl. 18.

191 Undulating green foliate line crossing a pair of thin black lines with magenta flowerlets at intersections. Main spray of green leaves and small polychrome flowerlets. Col. Pl. M.

195 Iron-red border line with swags of looped iron-red lines separated by mauve feathers and flowerlets with green leaves. Half-sun devices above swags. Main spray includes a mauve and a pink rose. Pl. 19.

196 142 Gold edge and inner gold line between which is a wavy line of blue and magenta ferns with large gold dot and gold dotted squiggles between.

198 Gold edge. Inner pair of gold lines with fleur-de-lis type devices dotted evenly between. A narrow band of gold foliage is close below the lower gold line.

199 (Unconfirmed.) Pink florets in gold medallions separated by gold elongated asterisk-like devices between parallel gold lines. Scattered gold dots and stars. (This number has also been seen on patt. 213.) Pl. 20.

200 Red and gold diamond belt with red and gold spoked oval medallions between parallel gold lines fringed with gold pendant. (Description as received.)

202 Gold edge and border lines. Wavy gold foliate band broken by dark blue and magenta flowerlets. Gold sprigs on body. Col. Pl. J.

206 167, 221–3, 227, 244, 254, 257, 258 Gold edge and border lines between which is a medium-sized yellow band. Gold sprigs on main body.

208 U39 Magenta edge. A black line with a line of blue arrowheads beneath; an undulating line of orange dots crosses the blue line. A long green leaf and two pink roses dominate the main spray. Col. Pl. G.

209 Gold chain and pendants looped from yellow band underlined in black between gold lines. Horizontal gold dashes above band. (Description as received.)

213 Gold edge and border lines. Gold broad-leaf sprays with florets in pale blue and a little magenta. This pattern has been seen marked 199. Col. Pl. K.

216 Gold edge. Narrow brown band containing single diamond with centre dot followed by a pair of white ovals repeated all round. Magenta swags are suspended from the diamonds.

221 167, 206, 222, 254, 257, 258 Gold edge and border lines with yellow band between edged in black and with a gold small leaf and berry edging.

222 167, 206, 221, 254, 257, 258 Gold edge and border lines. A broad pink border band beneath which is a line of small gold leaves and dots. Col. Pl. N.

223 229 Gold edge. Broad salmon-pink band with gold edge. Small scattered gold sprays.

227 167, 206, 221–3, 244, 254, 257, 258 Gold edge and border lines between which is a medium sized pink/apricot band. Gold sprigs on main body.

229 223 Gold edge. Broad raspberry pink band with gold edge. Small scattered gold sprays. Pl. 21.

230 Gold edge. Mazarine blue border overdecorated with formalized gold leaves and border. Inner decoration: mazarine blue and gold sprays.

231 Gold edge. Pink band with gold border from which runs a flattened S of gold dots to inner gold border, between these are two gold leaves and two magenta flowerlets. Pl. 22.

233 Gold edge and inner border between which are magenta scrolls with magenta and blue harebells. Pl. 23.

234 Gold edge and border line with mazarine blue band between with wavy gold line. Main decoration:

large single pink raspberries with single mazarine blue and pink flowers and stems overgilt. Green foliage. Pl. 24.

237 (Unconfirmed description.) Gold line border. A band of puce and blue flowers in white oval reserves separated by green trefoils. Polychrome scattered sprigs.

238 Gold edge and border band. A border of undulating gold foliage with magenta florets between a pair of thin and thick gold lines. Gold-edged pink ovals with gold centre dot are spaced along border. Pl. 25.

240 ?149 and 249 are identical. Gold edges and border lines. Narrow mazarine blue band overgilt with arrows and dots with below a further arched mazarine blue border with gold triangles, rising sun motifs and long pendants from points.

241 Black edge and border line. An undulating line of floral sprays is crossed by an undulating line of iron-red dots. The large floral main spray features a mauve and a pink rose with three pointed leaves. Col. Pls D and G.

243 251 Gold edge and border lines. Mazarine blue border overgilt with sideways on fleur-de-lis. Dot and dash line below, remainder is partially covered with gold scrollwork and leaf sprays. Col. Pl. M, Pl. 26.

244 167, 206, 221–3, 227, 254, 257, 258 Gold edge and border lines with a medium-sized royal blue band between. Gold sprigs on main body.

245 145 Gold edges and border lines from which hang large gold swags of foliage.

248 289, 301, 306, 307, 343, U230 Gold edge and border lines. Mazarine blue border band has arched and gilded lower edge from which hang three differing foliate pendants. Blue band is overgilt with a line of blobs and dots.

249 ?149 and 240 are identical! Gold edges and border lines. Narrow mazarine blue band overgilt with arrows and dots with below a further arched mazarine blue border with gold triangles, rising sun motifs, and long pendants from points.

251 243 Gold edge and border lines. Mazarine blue band overgilt with horizontal shuttlecock-shape leaf motif with intermediate dots. Gold dots and dashes beneath. Mazarine blue and gold sprigs. Pl. 27.

253 (Also in black with same number.) Iron-red border line and another line with mauve hearts and dots. Inner border is an undulating red line with mauve dots. Polychrome main spray features two roses. Polychrome sprigs.

254 167, 206, 221, 222, 257, 258 Gold edge and border lines. Gold-edged medium-width mole-coloured band. Spray of gold foliage above gold band. Pl. 28.

257 167, 206, 221, 222, 254, 258 Gold edge and border lines. Narrow black band with zigzag gold border below. Gold floral sprays.

258 167, 206, 221, 222, 254, 257 Gold edge and border lines. A dark pink band. Gold sprigs.

259 271, 275 Gold edge and border lines. Gold lattice work border band with either single red or blue dots within the lattice. Line of large and small dots under. Gold sprigs on body. See p. 81.

264 288, 280 Gold edge and border lines. Undulating gold line of small leaves and berries between two gold lines. Gold sprays and sprigs. See p. 81.

266 Gold edge and border lines. A border of two undulating and intersecting gold lines of leaves with red berries and small gold sprigs.

267 Magenta edge. A single undulating mauve line, alternate loops are filled with rose and other flower sprigs. Main spray is polychrome and features a single pink rose. Polychrome sprigs.

270 Gold edge and border line from which are suspended two sets of slightly different crossing gold swags. Base border line in gold. See p. 81.

271 259, 275 Gold edge. Gold inner border consisting of four parallel lines joined diagonally by similarly spaced lines so as to form parallelograms each fourth one being solid. Zigzag line and dots beneath. See p. 81.

272 274, 360, 490, 856, U93, U183, U301 Magenta edge. A narrow foliate band in two-tone blue broken by dotted red ovals. Main decoration is the 'tobacco' pattern with blue,

orange and green leaves and mauve flower. Wheel device orange and blue.

273 Pink scale border between iron-red lines with breaks for sprigs. Below is a mauve looped line and row of green and magenta sprigs. Main floral spray features a pink rose. Other polychrome sprigs. Col. Pls F and N.

274 272, 360, 490, 856, U93, U183, U301 Gold edge and border lines. 'Tobacco' pattern with leaves in dark blue and orange. The wheel-like device is in dotted orange. Some lesser green leaves. Complex top border. All overgilt.

275 259, 271 Gold edge. Gold inner border consisting of four parallel lines joined diagonally by similar lines to form parallelograms which are in sets, three in pink and one in gold. Gold zigzag line and dots under.

279 (Unconfirmed.) U297, 298 Pink edge. Narrow pink border line with pairs of small pink leaves and dots under. Main spray consists of pink rose right, two-tone mauve flower centre, four small orange flowers to left. Green foliage.

280 264, 288 Gold edge and border lines. Undulating line of small gold and black leaves with gold and magenta berries.

282 Gold edge and border lines. A border line of a single row of gold 'tadpoles'. See. p. 81.

283 64, 138, 175, 176 A border of two gold lines. Body decorated with scattered gold sprigs. See p. 81.

285 1018 Gold edge and border lines. A continuous border of a pair of strawberries then a triple leaf all in two-tone brown with gold foliage between a pair of gold lines. Gold sprigs.

288 264, 280 Gold edge and border lines between which is an undulating line of small gold leaves and orange berries. A few small gold and orange sprigs.

289 248, 301, 306, 307, 343, U230 Gold edge and border lines. Narrow orange band with arched gold band on lower edge from which hang uneven pairs of leafy stems in two different lengths all in gold.

290 Gold edge and border lines. A wide gold dense foliate border with mauve florets.

291 Gold edge and border lines between which is a gold dense foliate border with black and orange hips and single orange berries.

292 167, 206, 223, 227, 244, 254, 257, 258 Gold edge and border lines between which is a medium-sized orange band. Gold sprigs on main body.

294 295 Black edge and border line which has below a wavy line with small sprigs on it. Main floral spray, also in black, consists of a medium-sized flower with smaller flowers and foliage. Pl. 29.

295 294 All in iron-red. Edge and border line under which is a wavy line with small sprigs on it. Main floral spray consists of a medium-sized flower with smaller flowers and foliage. Pl. 30.

296 Border consists of two narrow iron-red bands with a green band between. Main decoration is usual pink rose spray. Col. Pl. N.

297 279, 298 Magenta edge. A narrow iron-red border overdecorated with zigzag white line and broken by floral sprays. Main spray features a large two-tone mauve flower with yellow centre and a pink rose.

298 279, 297 An iron-red and a mauve border line, under is a zigzag line with red rosebuds and mauve florets on it and blue dots. Main spray features a large two-tone mauve flower with yellow centre and a pink rose.

300 Gold edge and border lines between which is a fine narrow scrolled band of gold foliage with an occasional magenta flower. There are a few similar sprigs. See p. 81.

301 248, 289, 306, 307, 343, U230 Gold border lines and edge with arched band underneath from which hang uneven pairs of leafy stems in two different lengths. All gold.

302 329, 357, U87, U98 Gold edge and border lines. Band of brown oak leaves and acorns in pairs and singles, all but one facing outwards, overgilt.

303 Gold edge and border lines. Gold wavy vine border with bunches of grapes.

306 248, 289, 301, 307, 343, U230
Gold edge and border lines. Medium-size blue band under which is a decorative arched gold band with hatching and foliate pendants of two different lengths. Col. Pl. K.

307 248, 289, 301, 306, 343, U230
Gold edge and border lines. Narrow purple band under which is a decorative arched gold band with hatching and foliate pendants of two different lengths.

308 328 All black decoration. Border is a line, a dotted line, two lines and an undulating line with occasional sprigs attached. Main decoration is a high-handled plain basket of flowers with ribbon on handle.

311 A broad cross-hatched pink border band, edged in iron-red with a dashed and a plain iron-red line above. Border is broken by round and irregular cartouches containing floral sprays. Sprigs. Pl. 31.

312 Magenta edge, iron-red border line. A narrow slightly wavy border of mauve feathers broken by pink and green sprigs. Main polychrome spray features a pink rose, a bud, and three puce pansies.

313 (Not confirmed.) Gold edge and border lines. Orange band with gold edges overdecorated with an irregular wavy gold line. Border is split by a gilt leaf device. A few small gold sprigs on body. Pl. 32.

314 318 Gold edge and border lines. A band of undulating gold foliage with orange flowers and buds between

a plain gold line and a gold line with a wavy gold line crossing it.

316 Gold edge and border lines. An orange-brown band of semicircles outlined and overdecorated in black and connected by loops of black dots. Gold foliate pendants and groups of three black berries.

317 Gold edge and border lines between which is a broad band of closely spaced gold flowers, orange flowers and mauve leaves with some lesser foliage.

318 314 Gold edge and border lines. A broad band of undulating gold foliage with pink flowers and buds beneath the gold edge. Underneath is a gold line crossed by a wavy gold line.

319 Gold edge and thin gold line connected to, and by, a similar pair so as to form a divided border containing two bunches of dark purple grapes and gold foliage in one part and a blue flower spray in the next. Col. Pl. J.

323 Gold edge and border lines. Between a pair of gold lines is an undulating gold line with alternate small sprigs and blobs. There is a single gold star within each undulation. Gold arrowhead line under. See p. 81.

324 Gold border line. Brown floral sprays and sprigs overgilt.

326 All gold decoration. Edge and border lines between which is a narrow wavy stem line with alternate single multipointed leaves and single berries. See p. 81.

328 308 Border is an iron-red line, a dotted line, two lines, and an undulating dotted line with occasional sprigs attached. A high handled plain iron-red basket of polychrome flowers with ribbon on handle.

329 302, 357, U87, U98 Gold edge and border lines. Between gold lines an undulating band of triple oak leaves alternating with four acorns. Overgilt. Pl. 33.

330 Gold edge and border line between which is an undulating line of gold foliage with large single magenta harebells.

331 Gold edge and border line. A gold band formed by a pair of broad and narrow lines between which is a wavy tendril of hips. A further zigzag line of small three-pointed leaves. Pl. 34.

334 Gold edge and border lines. Mazarine blue band with zigzag gold leaves and dots. Mazarine blue twigs with leaves in iron-red, green, gold, and mazarine blue with gold outlines. Faint iron-red flowers. Pl. 35.

336 Blue edge and border lines. Scattered blue sprigs. Pl. 36.

338 Mauve border line has loops attached. A double dot undulating mauve line is broken by floral sprays. A disc of polychrome segments is surrounded by a narrow polychrome floral garland.

339 Gold edge and border line. A broad border, mainly in gold, of fern-like leaves in < formation with a few florets in blue and magenta. A thin gold stem with magenta berries forms bottom of border.

342 This seems to be any blue and white border pattern with any polychrome floral spray or sprig pattern added. Possible gold edge.

343 248, 289, 301, 306, 307, U230 Gold edge and border lines. A blue border band is overdecorated alternately top and bottom with three gold leaves. Beneath is a gold band of arches and pendant foliage in two lengths. Pl. 37.

344 546, 547 Gold edges. Black rose sprigs dotted all over.

346 Gold edge and border lines between which are suspended undulating gold foliate sprays with magenta hips.

347 Gold edge and border lines between which is a border of gold edged brown circles containing formalized white flower-heads and separated by gold fronds. There is a looped gold line beneath. Pl. 38.

348 Gold edge and inner notched border line between which are groups of dark brown leaves with gold foliage and dark brown hips separating them.

349 Gold edge and border lines between which is an undulating line of gold foliage with bunches of mauve hips. Below lower border line is a line of gold loops with pendants. Pl. 39.

350 Gold edge and border line. A slightly undulating stem of brown elderberry tendrils. A gold herring-bone band beneath. Pl. 40.

351 Gold edge and lower gold line between which is a row of mauve discs joined by an undulating feathery line and flowerlets etc. all in gold. Dotted gold sprigs and lower gold border line. Pl. 41.

353 Pale magenta edge band with loops under. A border or magenta sprays connected by a line. A chain in mauve and green. Main spray features pink and mauve flowers with two-tone green leaves. Pl. 42.

354 746, 791 Magenta edge. Black border line with pink scale blobs separated by polychrome sprigs. A thin line of magenta arrowheads. Small polychrome floral sprays.

356 Gold edge and border lines between which is a band of single large orange flowers separated by groups of four dark green oak leaves, brown acorns, and gold foliage. Pl. 43.

357 302, 329, U87, U98 Gold edge and inner line of small zigzag leaves. A band of a pair of oak leaves alternating with a single oak leaf all in two-tone green and separated by three brown and tan acorns with brown tendrils. Pl. 44.

360 272, 274, 490, 856, U93, U183, U301 Gold edge and border lines. Commonly known as 'tobacco' pattern. Leaves: dark blue, orange, and yellow. The wheel-like device is in orange and yellow with a white centre. Complex top border. Overgilt.

362 Gold edge and border lines between which are pink daisy heads on gold discs separated by magenta triangles at top and by undulating gold foliage with magenta flowers. Zigzag gold line beneath.

363 365 Gold edge and border lines. A border of sprays of gold foliage with four mauve flowers and buds. Inner wavy gold border line.

365 363 Gold edge and border lines within which is a border of alternating up-and-down gold sprays with four small orange flowers and buds. Beneath is a small zigzag gold border with dots.

366 Magenta edge. Two iron-red border lines from which are alternately suspended polychrome floral cornucopias and small floral sprays tied with ribbon. There are similar sprays on the main body.

367 598, 599 All black decoration. Edge line. Undulating dotted line with sprigs at every other wave. Inner wavy border of 'tadpoles'. Floral spray with central rose and other lesser flowers.

369 Gold edges and border lines. A gold band of two leaves and two berries alternating. A gold line with magenta 'sunsets' above and below alternately separated by an undulating line of gold leaves.

373 Gold edge and border line. Iron-red border line with small loops, dots and pendants beneath is broken by a large mauve bloom which is joined by green foliage to other flowers. Similar to famille rose.

376 A border of pink rose sprays joined by a line. A similar central polychrome spray plus a number of scattered mauve sprigs.

377 Magenta edge and border line. Main spray features a blue-petalled flower outlined in magenta with yellow centre and a number of brown buds outlined with black dots. The leaves are two-tone green. Blue sprigs.

378 Edge band of pink arrowheads between black lines. Undulating stem of green violet leaves alternating with magenta flowerlets entwined about a straight line. Pl. 45.

379 382 Black edge. Brown band edged in black and overdecorated with diagonal black leaf sprays. Zigzag orange line with black crosses on it.

381 Black border line. Border is two broken crossing wavy lines of fine black foliage. Pl. 46.

382 379 Dark brown edge. Apple-green band edged in black and overdecorated with diagonal black leaf sprays. Zigzag orange line with black crosses on it.

393 Mole coloured border lines and sparse floral sprays. Pl. 47.

394 Gold edge and border lines. A broad undulating line of gold foliage with two or three colour flowers in magenta, yellow, and black. Pl. 48.

398 Gold edge and border lines with inner dotted lines and similar joining

lines to form cartouches which contain a complex pink geometric pattern, two mauve blooms and two magenta flowers alternately.

401 Black edge and border lines. A border of black leaves with hips below. A border of joined black curve ended oblongs each containing a * device. Pl. 49.

408 498 Gold edge and border lines. The mazarine blue band has gilt edges and beneath are small gold pendants and dots. The band is overgilt with a wavy line of small three-pronged leaves. Col. Pl. K.

411 Gold edge and border lines. Mazarine blue band overgilt with two connected rows of squiggles, dots, and circles. Beneath is a line of gold loops and dots. Gold sprigs on main body. Pl. 50.

415 Blue edge. A border of green swags on black lines crossed by similar yellow swags. Each intervening space has a blue dot.

420 430, 515 Black edge. A border of black wheat ears in a wavy line formation.

421 431 Oriental scene known as the boy with the butterfly. The main figure is in blue, and the other two in magenta and green. Blue butterfly. Col. Pl. C.

422 Gold edge and border line. A border of blue florets interspersed with broader magenta florets. Main body decorated with sprays of a blue flower with magenta leaves.

423 Gold border bands with fine gold line beneath the top band. Central black and white floral spray and several sprigs. Pl. 51.

425 1066 Gold edge and border line. Heavily decorated polychrome border with oriental scene known as the window pattern. Col. Pl. B.

426 Gold edge with fine gold line beneath and lower gold border. A central spray of three pink flowers backed by three green leaves with veins and a yellow flower with blue/green leaves. Gilt sprays.

427 Gold edges and border lines. Mazarine blue band is overgilt with interlocking gold ovals with three dots in each. Col. Pl. J.

428 534 Gold edge. Gold border line with trefoils alternating either side. Undulating gold stem with pairs of leaves alternating with a curved-stem rose hip either side.

430 420, 515 Gold edge and border line. Border of very dark brown wheat ears which are in a wavy line formation. Pl. 52.

431 421 Boy with the butterfly pattern but with the main figure dressed in yellow and mauve instead of blue.

433 467 All black version of patt. 467. Narrow border of a pair of lines with circles between. A pair of lines is crossed by an undulating ribbon with interspersed sprigs. Main spray has a large flower.

434 Brown edge. A border of blue-petalled flowers outlined in iron-red with the tendrils and the rest of the foliage also mainly in iron-red. The lesser flowers and leaves are picked out in blue or green. Pl. 53.

435 436 Gold edges and border lines. A border of rectangular cartouches with blue vertical dividers alternately containing hand-painted rural scenes and gold diamonds. Zigzag gold twig border under.

436 435 Gold edges and border lines. A border of rectangular cartouches with mauve vertical dividers alternately containing hand-painted rural scenes and gold diamonds. Zigzag gold twig border under. Pl. 54.

437 Gold edge and border line. A continuous slightly wavy stem of gold leaves makes up the border. (Stem may also be in mauve. See Holgate in Bibliography.) Pl. 55.

439 Gold edge. Narrow overgilt orange band crossed by undulating gold band of foliage. Small orange and gold sprays alternate above and below.

441 Gold edge, inner line and border. A border consisting of an undulating line of foliage mainly in gold but with some parts in black and orange.

442 Magenta border band. Iron-red line under which is a border of separated sprays of flowers, one in orange, two ferns in dotted iron-red, one magenta and two blue flowers, green leaves. Other sprigs.

443 521, U113 (See also 443a.) Gold edge and border lines. Large six-pointed feather-like leaf in dotted black and red, similar smaller leaves and red and black hips all overgilt. Gold tendrils and zigzag lines. Pl. 56.

443a (Unconfirmed alternative description of patt. 443.) Gold edge. Border consists of groups of five fern leaves in dotted black and gold interspersed with a similar five-pointed leaf and a mauve leafy spray. Gold tendrils and zigzag lines.

444 89 (Unconfirmed.) Gold edge and border lines. A border of large gold ovals each containing a black lily and joined by dots at interstices.

445 Gold edge and border lines. The mainly gold border consists of dark blue, orange (?pink) edged, with gold leaves, fuchsia-type single flowers. Gold sprigs on body.

446 Gold edge and border lines. A mazarine blue stunted tree with orange fruits and dotted orange leaves all heavily outlined in gold. Col. Pl. K, Pl. 57.

449 Iron-red edge line from which hang polychrome floral swags with half sunburst devices above. The main floral spray features two magenta roses and is framed by a wavy magenta line. Col. Pls G and N.

450 Magenta edge line. An undulating purple dotted line is crossed by an undulating foliate line. A straight magenta line with loops under. Main spray features a pink and a mauve rose and some blue flowers.

451 Gold edge and border lines. A vine border comprising pairs of mauve bunches of grapes separated by three leaves all connected by gold stems and tendrils.

455 Also in black and red. Gold edge and border line. The rest of the decoration in shades of orange consists of drape-like swags with bows at the top from which hang tasselled ribbons. Pl. 58.

459 554 Golden edge and border lines. A broad orange band overdecorated with gold scrollwork. Underneath is a line of alternate gold crosses and dots. Pl. 59.

461 Black edge and border line. Black floral sprays.

462 466, 511, 709, 1063, 1100 Gold edge and border line. Inner border of pairs of gold leaves alternating with pairs of berries on stalks. Black and white rural prints. Pl. 60.

465 Patt. no. refers to gilding. Blue and white two insect pattern with gilt foliate line border.

466 462, 511, 709, 1063 Gold edge and border lines between which is a broad band of scrolled leaves interspersed with cross devices. Black and white rural prints.

467 433 A narrow border of black lines with iron-red circles between. Two iron-red lines are crossed by an undulating iron-red ribbon with interspersed sprigs. Polychrome spray features a magenta flower. Pl. 61.

469 Wide blue band carrying chain of gold ovals (gold hyphen centres) gold trefoils at links, undulating foliate line behind. (Description as received.)

471 Gold edge with a hatched and arched band beneath from which hang gold foliate sprays with blue and red flowerlets.

472 Gold edge. A broad black border band is overdecorated with curved panels which are magenta colour at the left end fading to white at the right end. Each panel contains a black leaf spray.

473 Refers to gilding only. Blue and white twisted tree pattern with gold edge. Row of dots and dashes between gold lines from the lower of which hang single leaves at an angle.

475 (See also 475a.) Gold edge and border lines. Highly decorative gold inner border. Large Greek key pattern band in orange and black. Flattened Greek key pattern in gold. Pl. 62.

475a (Query wrong patt. no – reported alternative description of patt. 475.) Gilt foliage borders. Black bat-printed panels of rural scenes.

478 586 Gold edge and border line. Inner border of a continuous wavy gold sprig supporting mauve and black hips in groups of three above and below.

480 Gold edge and border lines. An undulating gold line with single leaves and two berries crosses a straight gold line. Gold floral spray.

484 Gold edge and border lines. Main motif is large palm trees with nuts in mazarine blue, orange, and gold. Similarly coloured large flowers.

487 559 Gold edge and border lines. Highly decorative inner gold border. Main decoration is a blue rural scene print. Pl. 63.

490 272, 274, 360, 856, U93, U183, U301 Gold edge and border lines. Mazarine blue border with zigzag gold leaves and dots. 'Tobacco' pattern with blue, orange, and gold leaves. The blue-edged wheel device is white with gold and magenta centre. Col. Pl. J.

495 Gold edge. Inner border of two types of gold leaves in arrowhead formation. Main decoration is a sepia classical print. Pl. 64.

498 408 (Possible misnumbering.) Gold edge and border lines. The mazarine blue band has gilt edges and beneath are small gold pendants and dots. The band is overgilt with a wavy line of small three-pronged leaves.

499 Gold edge and border lines. Broad mazarine blue border is decorated with white blooms which have gold and orange centres. Remainder of border is overdecorated with gold scroll work.

503 Rim of single puce trefoils separated by gilding between gold lines. (Description as received.)

504 505 Broad orange band overgilded with diamonds alternately containing a wreath and parallel lines with three discs. Each diamond overlaps the next to it. Edges and borders are also gold.

505 504 Broad mazarine blue band overgilded with diamonds alternately containing a wreath and parallel lines with three discs. Each diamond overlaps the next to it. Edges and borders are also gold.

510 Highly gilt 'Japan' type pattern with border band of rectangular cartouches in orange and blue. Main decoration comprises a fence and flowers in iron-red and mazarine blue. Pl. 65.

511 462, 466, 709, 1063 Gold edge, broad band of gold scrollwork with line of gold dots beneath. Black and white rural print.

515 420, 430 Gold edge and border line. Border of blue wheat ears in wavy line formation.

516 Gold diamond medallions between horizontal gold plumes on rust band. (Description as received.)

520 Polychrome oriental scene in a courtyard with a figure in doorway on the right, another in window to the left, and two in foreground; one carries a tea bowl and saucer. Scene through oval in rear wall.

521 443, U113 Gold edge and border lines. Large seven-pointed feather like leaf and other lesser leaves in dotted orange with orange berries overgilt and with gold stems. Gold tendrils and zigzag lines.

524 Gold edge and border lines. A narrow line of gold leaves alternating either side. A broad band comprised of an undulating stem with single large mazarine blue leaves, single acorns, and gold foliage.

527 Gold edge and border lines. Broad mazarine blue border over-decorated with pairs of large white and gold leaves with single berry. Gold scrolls and tendrils between.

533 Gold edge and border lines. Broad mazarine blue band overdecorated with green and yellow bunches of grapes, gold tendrils, and vine leaves.

536 636 Gold edges and border. Wavy border of gold leaves and pairs of berries. Mazarine blue border overgilt with two rows of trefoils, thin zigzag line, and dots. A similar inner gold border on the white.

538 Mazarine blue background over-gilt with a design of four parallel lines which cross and form a geometric pattern of right angles with interspersed single oak leaves and acorns.

540 Gold edge and border bands. Broad mazarine blue band overdecorated with simple white leaves and harebells which are themselves overgilt. Pl. 66.

541 Black-edged narrow iron-red border band with magenta scale areas beneath. Main motif is a tall iron-red vase with decorative bands filled with a polychrome bunch of flowers and foliage.

542 Gold edges and border lines. Main decoration is a single wavy line which also undulates and has occasional small sprays attached all in gold. See p. 82.

543 545 Gold edges and inner band. Two narrow parallel lines with row of dots and dashes between from which hang inverted swags with single many-pointed leaves at junctions, all in two-tone orange.

544 (Not confirmed.) Brown edge. Narrow border line of single two-tone green leaves separated by small iron-red sprays.

545 543 Gold edges and inner band. Two narrow parallel lines with row of dots and dashes between from which hang inverted swags with single many-pointed leaves at junctions, all in two-tone brown. Pl. 67.

546 344, 547 Gold edges. Orange coloured rose sprigs dotted all over.

547 344, 546 Gold edges. Iron-red coloured rose sprigs dotted all over. Pl. 68.

550 761 Gold edges and border lines. Main overall decoration is orange tendrils with large mazarine blue exotic animals with long curly tails, large mazarine blue leaves, and stems all heavily overgilt. Very fine. Pl. 69.

551 651 Gold edge and border lines. Broad mazarine blue band overdecorated with a gold sprig band and a pair of gold and white interwoven ribbons. Interspersed sprigs. Pl. 70.

553 (?Mismarked, 556 identical.) Gold edge. Border of two gold bands with between them a line of white squares, quartered, on their corners and shaded between. Remainder mazarine blue overgilt with simple leaves and twigs.

554 459 Gold edge and border lines. A broad mazarine blue band overdecorated with gold scrollwork. Underneath is a line of alternate gold crosses and dots. Col. Pl. H.

555 Wide scrolled ribbon with red feathers on black band. (Description as received.)

556 553 Gold edge. Border of two gold bands with between them a line of white squares, quartered, on their corners and shaded between. Remainder mazarine blue overgilt with simple leaves and twigs. Pl. 71.

557 Gold border. Overall decoration of large and small mauve flowers on brown branch with overgilt green, orange and brown leaves, and orange and brown buds. Pl. 72.

558 695 Gold edge and border lines. Broad orange band decorated with a line of single gold-edged trefoil white leaves joined by gold tendrils. Pl. 73.

559 487 Gold edges. A border of three lines of gold devices. A black and white rural scene is enclosed in a rectangular cartouche formed by gold band top and bottom and stylized wheatsheaf either side.

562 Gold edge. Overall decoration of mazarine blue oak leaves, acorns, and flowers all overgilt and separated by gold fronds and tendrils. Pl. 74.

563 Gold edge. Mazarine blue background is overgilded with foliate scrolls and individual formalized flower-heads in two sizes.

565 Underglaze blue ground, gilded embellishments. Gold swirling leaf stems with spade-shaped leaves gilded in reserves. (Description as received.)

566 Gold edge. Very broad mazarine blue band overdecorated with large white leaf which has gold scroll work and intricate edges. There is further gold scroll work and smaller leaves etc. on the blue band. Pl. 75.

568 Gold edge and border lines. Border of single fern leaves of which one half is iron-red and the other gold placed at an angle and interspersed with similarly coloured fine foliage. Similar sprigs. Pl. 76.

569 Gold edge and border lines. Band of close-packed narrow gold leaves in arrow formation. Mazarine blue border overgilt with single heart-shaped leaves joined by wavy stem with other fronds. Pl. 77.

570 572, 752, U152, U177 Gold edges and border of gold harebell shapes. Chinese-style scene, central beehive. Building and tree to right, floral plant left. Main colour mazarine blue wih orange heavily overgilt. Pl. 78.

571 Gold edges and borders. Broad mazarine blue border with oval

cartouches each containing a single rose or other flower with foliage. Between cartouches are single gilt flowers and foliage.

572 570, 752, U152 (Not confirmed.) Gold edges. Border of gold harebell shapes. Chinese-style scene of central beehive, building and tree to right, floral bush to left. Main colours are mazarine blue and orange heavily overgilt.

575. Gold edges and border lines. Gold border of thin harebell-like devices. Broad arched mazarine blue border overgilt with tendrils. Arches contain discs or diamonds with gold scroll work. Pl. 79.

581. Gold edge and border bands. Broad mazarine blue band overgilded with decorated spiral scrollwork.

583 Gold edge and border lines. Two mazarine blue borders overdecorated in zigzag gold joined by similar diagonal lines so as to form cartouches containing gilt ferns.

585 Gold edge. Decoration in mazarine blue and gold consists of a line of spade-shaped leaves each joined to the next by an S in the middle of which is a ring of six circles. Gold fern leaves fill spaces.

586 478 Gold edge and border line. Inner border of a continuous wavy gold sprig supporting orange and black hips in groups of three above and below. Pl. 80.

593 Magenta edge. Narrow blue border of alternate cross-hatching with magenta scroll inserts. Main central spray is of one large pink flower and smaller flowers in yellow, mauve, and blue. Green leaves. Pl. 81.

594 R Iron-red edge border of a line and cross devices. Border spray of large crudely-painted flowers in pink, iron-red, and yellow. Several smaller single flower sprays all with two-tone green leaves. Pl. 82.

596 Iron-red border line with magenta line under from which are suspended swags of magenta arrow-heads and green ovals with double pendants at alternate junctions. Main spray has large magenta flower. Pl. 83.

597 Mazarine blue and gold Greek key pattern.

598 367, 599 All orange decoration. Edge line. Undulating dotted line with sprigs at every other wave. Inner wavy border of 'tadpoles'. Floral spray with central rose and other lesser flowers.

599 367, 598 Black edge line. Undulating dotted iron-red line with alternate polychrome sprigs. Inner wavy border line of iron-red 'tadpoles'. Central pink rose spray.

603 Magenta edge line. Border of pairs of dark brown leaves separated by floral sprigs and occasional sprays. Main spray has a mauve and a magenta rose and several smaller flowers and green leaves.

604 (Refers to gilding.) Blue and white twisted tree pattern overgilt as

follows: edge and border line, two thin lines close together with line of blobs between, beneath is a broad band of short and long angled slashes.

605 140 Pink border band is magenta-edged with magenta-edged ogee diagonals separated by four dots. There is a zigzag line below the lower edge line. Main spray has single pink rose and green leaves.

611 Gold edges and border line. Narrow gilt edged mazarine blue border. Mazarine and light blue truncated cone-shaped basket with overgilding filled with pink, orange, and blue flowers with shaded green foliage.

614 All gold decoration. Dentil edge. Border band of sheaves of leaves connected by a wavy dotted line with two large dots which are themselves joined by a fernlike scroll. Thick and thin border line. See p. 82.

619 Monochrome design in iron red. Border consists of 'coolie hat' shaped devices interspersed with almost plain tapered bands. Central motif of single maple leaves and other leaves.

621 673 Magenta scale border broken by large orange and small round white cartouches containing sprigs. Oriental scene with mainly blue and yellow figures sometimes known as 'dinner is served'.

622 Mazarine blue ground. Large four-petalled flower with large single fuzzy leaves in gold. (Description as received.)

623 Gold edges and border lines. Broad mazarine blue band decorated with large and medium white and gold daisies overgilt with scrollwork.

625 Gold edge. Monochrome orange design consists of a broad border with white rough semicircular cut-outs and white dotted fern leaves. Centre has a number of flying bat-shaped devices.

629 (Not confirmed.) Mazarine blue ground overgilt and decorated with large pink strawberries.

630 Gold edges and border lines. Main motif is of a spray of four large leaves of different shapes in mazarine blue with over gilding. Gold twigs between.

631 Gold edge and border lines. Mazarine blue decoration consists of vine stems with bunches of grapes and vine leaves all over gilt. Pl. 84.

636 536 Gold edges and border. Mazarine blue border overgilt with two rows of trefoils, thin zigzag line and dots. There is a similar inner gold border on the white. Col. Pl. K.

638 Gold edge and border lines. Inner mazarine blue border overgilt with many-pointed leaf design. On either side are two further borders of a thin wavy leaf design. Very high quality. Pl. 85.

644 Gold edge and border lines. Single large mazarine blue blackberry leaves separated by five berries all heavily overgilded and connected by gold tendrils. Pl. 86.

645 Gold edges. Main decoration consists of vine leaves in mazarine blue and gold on mazarine blue stems with bunches of gold grapes.

647 Gold edges and border lines. White border. Remainder covered in multicoloured marble effect.

651 551 Gold edge and border lines. Broad orange band overdecorated with a gold sprig band and a pair of gold and white interwoven ribbons. Interspersed sprigs. Pl. 87.

653 Gold edges and border lines. Mazarine blue background overgilt with laurel leaves and with gold-edged oval cartouches which have a dotted orange border and central white leaf on gold background. Pl. 88.

657 248, 289, 301, 306, 307, 343 (Not confirmed.) Gold edge and border lines. The mazarine blue border band is overdecorated with gold ovals with central dots. Beneath is a gold band of hatched arches and pendant foliage in two lengths.

660 748 Iron-red border line. A border of single fan-like blue flowers separated by small floral sprays with tendrils. Several polychrome sprigs and a main spray with a single magenta rose and green leaves. Pl. 89.

662 Magenta edge line. Narrow orange border band broken by small floral cartouches, overdecorated with white zigzag line, loops and blue trefoils under. Main spray has two large magenta flowers and others. Pl. 90.

669 Gold edge and border lines. Broad mazarine border straight on one side and wavy on the other overgilt with a star-burst centred flower and heavy leafy scrollwork.

670 692 Gold edge and border lines. Broad orange band overgilt with a continuous spray of leaves and tendrils. Pl. 91.

671 Wide mazarine blue band embellished with gold passion-flower and foliage plus oval insets of differing hand-painted flowers.

672 Gold edge and border lines. Broad orange band overdecorated with large green leaf and three white flowers with yellow centres. Beneath and surrounding these is a continuous spray of gold foliage. Pl. 92.

673 621 Edge band consists of a narrow row of iron-red circles between black lines. Gold foliate border broken by cartouches filled with flowers or scenes. Oriental scene known as 'dinner is served'. Pl. 93.

675 Gilded rust ground, three oak leaves divided lengthways into green and yellow, three trios of open star-shaped flower-heads reserved. (Description as received.)

676 Gold edge and border lines. Very broad orange border overdecorated with square white daisies, small white leaves, small white squares with central crosses, and heavy gold scrollwork. Pl. 94.

678 (Description not confirmed.) Gold, orange, and white floral decoration.

686 Pink scale border band between iron-red lines. A further band of small arched loops below straight line. Main spray features two large back-to-back flowers in puce and magenta.

692 670 Gold edge and border lines. Broad mazarine blue band overgilt with a continuous spray of leaves and tendrils.

695 558 Gold edge and border lines. Broad mazarine blue band decorated with a line of single gold-edged trefoil white leaves joined by gold tendrils.

699 Stipple print. Flower baskets, different front and back. Separate flower sprigs. No rim band. (Description as received.)

709 462, 466, 511, 1063 Black edge. Black and white print of rural scene.

735 Wide mazarine blue ground with heavy gold ogees and ferns. (Description as received.)

736 Gold edge and border lines. Broad mazarine blue band decorated with overlapping white semicircles with gold edges and central chain with gold swags beneath and formalized gold flower and leaves above.

737 Gold edges and border bands. Orange bunches of berries/grapes with mazarine blue leaves all overgilded. Gold tendrils.

738 Gold edge. Pairs of orange strawberries with mazarine blue leaves and stalks all overgilt and with gold tendrils. Pl. 95.

744 709, 1063 Black edge and border lines above and below black and white prints of rural scenes.

746 354, 791 Broad pink scale border broken by two sizes of polychrome floral cartouches. Main decoration is a brown basket with a polychrome bouquet of flowers.

747 434 Black edge and decoration. Border of eight-pointed single flowers each bordered on either side by a twisted tendril from which sprouts one stalk with two pairs of small flowers and leaves.

748 660 Iron-red border line. A border of single fan-like iron-red flowers separated by small floral sprays with tendrils. Several polychrome sprigs and a main spray with a single magenta rose, green leaves.

749 Magenta border comprises a straight line with narrow wavy line of scrolls beneath and pendant flowers with long stamens. Main spray is a pink rose with foliage. Other double daisy/rose sprigs.

752 570, 572, U152 Gold edge and gold border line between which is a continuous wavy line of fruit and leaves. Oriental type scene. Central beehive, building and tree right. Mazarine blue, light blue, and orange. Overgilt.

753 Gold edges and border lines. Inner wavy line border of continuous leaf sprays. Black and white fruit print.

760 Gold edge. Border of crossing wavy lines of stalks with small leaves all in iron-red. (Also in black.) Pl. 96.

761 550 Gold edges and border lines. Main overall colour is mazarine blue with light blue spots. Main decoration is exotic animals with long curly tails, large leaves with stems, all in gold and white. Fine quality. Col. Pl. A.

762 Gold edge and border bands. Broad orange band decorated with a line of gold-edged and half-garlanded white trefoil leaves alternately inverted and connected by gold scrolls. Pl. 97.

763 Gold edges and border lines. Broad orange border overdecorated with single green leaves, pink strawberries with gold foliage and tendrils.

764 All mauve decoration.

770 Gold edge and border lines. Very broad orange border overdecorated with groups of seven small white daisies and large sprays of three green leaves plus foliate overgilding.

771 Gold border lines. Broad orange band overdecorated with undulating white stem of individual and differing large white flowers with yellow stamens etc., yellow and green leaves. Tendril overgilding. Pl. 98.

775 Gold edge and border lines. Two bands in mazarine blue overgilt with three rows of dashes. There is a wavy line of blue devices of differing sizes and gold scrolls between the bands.

777 Gold edge and border lines. Inner gold leaf border. Broad mazarine blue band overdecorated with rough cogwheel-like devices in white, light blue, and orange. All edges and spaces are highly gilt.

779 Gold edge and border lines. Broad mazarine blue band decorated with white vine leaves and yellow bunches of grapes all overgilt.

780 Border with gold line edges contains a line of a single flower and two buds in mazarine blue with gilt fern like foliage.

781 Gold edges and border lines. Broad central band comprised of large three-sectioned leaves and acorns in mazarine blue and gold with lesser gold foliage. Col. Pl. H.

783 All decoration in iron-red. Edge line, border of three rows of miniature trident heads, then a thin line followed by a thin wavy line with fern-like appendages.

786 Gold edge and highlights. A border band of puce leaves in arrowhead formation with single berry stalks between. A few puce and gold sprigs on main body.

789 Gold edge. Highly decorative gold border of various cartouches containing scenes. Chinese scene of seated blue figure holding box, up to five other figures in yellow, blue, and magenta outside buildings. Pl. 99.

790 Gold edges and border lines. Narrow border chain of differing blue flowers and green foliage. Similar sprigs dotted about.

791 354, 746 Edge has two narrow black lines with iron-red devices between. Inner pink scale border with large and small cartouches containing floral sprays. Central bouquet of different coloured flowers.

794 Gold edge and border lines. Either a large pink rose with two-tone green leaves, gold fern fronds and tendrils or a flame marigold with two-tone green leaves and gold leafy sprays. Pl. 100.

798 Monochrome magenta decoration. Border band of overlapping circles and dots. The lower foliate border line has the larger leaves angled on the under side. Pl. 101.

799 Iron-red border line. Narrow band of iron-red scrolls between individual pink roses. Main spray mainly comprised of a single pink rose and green leaves.

810 Gold edges and border lines. Broad band in mazarine blue dotted with gold and decorated with large white leaves and oval cartouches with gold sprays all edged in gold. Further gold leaf spray border. Pl. 102.

812 Gold edge and border lines. Mazarine blue band with large single orange flowers interspersed with three white leaves all overgilt.

822 827 (Not confirmed.) Gold edge and border lines. Two mazarine blue bands overgilt with dots connected by similar vertical bands to form cartouches containing sprays with pale pink and black trefoils and gold leaves.

824 826 is almost identical. Gold edge and inner gold line enclosing narrow mazarine blue and gilt band. Inner irregular border in mazarine blue, blue, and orange comprising leaves, sunrise device, and central sprays all overgilt. Pl. 103.

826 824 is almost identical. Two gold lines enclosing narrow mazarine blue and gilt band. Inner irregular border in mazarine blue, blue, and orange comprising leaves, sunrise device, and central sprays all overgilt. Pl. 104.

827 822 Gold edge and border lines. Two mazarine blue bands overgilt with dots connected by similar vertical bands to form cartouches containing sprays with orange and black trefoils and gold leaves.

829 1270, 1415 Gold edge and borders. All-over pattern of mazarine blue strawberry leaves, natural strawberries all overgilded, and gold tendrils. Col. Pl. H.

830 420, 430, 515 Gold edge and border line. Inner border of single gold dots. An arched line of gold stems, tendrils, and leaves supports the dark blue overgilded barley ears which have iron-red beards.

835 Gold edge and border lines. Broad mazarine blue border crossed at an angle by wide wavy gold-edged white lines. Mazarine blue is overgilt with sprigs.

838 Edge border of small black circles. Inner border of black line crossed by a wavy black line with two tiny offshoots. Mauve, yellow, and green floral spray outlined in black. Pl. 105.

839 Iron-red border line. Undulating foliate border line with green leaves, single magenta florets alternating with pairs of blue dotted florets. A few floral sprigs on body.

840 888, (846 similar. Query number). Gold edge and border lines. Broad overgilt mazarine blue band near centre between large cartouches of Warburtons Patent rural scenes. Outstanding quality. Pl. 106.

846 888 (840 similar. Query number). Gold edges and border lines. Mazarine blue band overdecorated with a wavy line of gold foliage. Warburtons Patent gold rural print with predominant figures.

856 272, 274, 360, 490, U93, U183, U301 Gold edge and border line with gold foliate band between. 'Tobacco' pattern, mazarine blue background, leaves: white, orange, and green. White wheel device has blue spokes. All is heavily gilt.

874 Orange print. Blue rim. Border and gold bouquet of convolvulus. (Description as received.)

876 1054, 1163, 2359 Gold edge and border line between which is a wavy gold line with vertical dashes. Chinese-style scene in mazarine blue, light blue, and orange of an elephant to right, a tree and buildings all overgilt. Pl. 107.

880 Gold edge and border lines. Broad mazarine blue band with a row of large white flowers and berries overgilt and with gold tendrils.

881 Gold border lines between which is a row of mazarine blue oak leaves alternating with acorns and gold twiglets. All overgilt.

882 Gold edge and border lines. Broad mazarine blue band overgilded with narrow leaves and broken by a line of curved-edge diamond devices with gold central motif and edges. Pl. 108.

885 Gold edge and border lines between which is a broad mazarine blue band overdecorated with one large and three smaller simple white flowers with yellow centres and separated by gold foliage. Pl. 109.

888 840, 846 Gold edge and border lines. Broad mazarine blue band high up overdecorated with gold foliage. Warburtons Patent rural scenes. Outstanding quality. Pl. 110.

901 Gold edge and border lines. Broad undulating line of gold foliage with single blue and orange flowers placed in zigzag fashion above and below the foliate line.

911 Blue edge. Overall sprigs in blue, orange, and yellow, also black kite-tail sprigs.

914 Gold edge and border lines. Broad border of single large pink roses separated by large spray of green leaves.

919 (Possibly 616.) Gold edge. Orange-red background overdeco-rated with large gold-edged white heart-shaped devices containing gold leaves. The spaces between contain single large gold leaves and tendrils. See p. 82.

921 Gold edge and border lines. Broad mazarine blue band with large white convolvulus flowers, green leaves, and gold sprigs. Lower gold border of pairs of leaves alternating with pairs of berries.

922 Gold edge and border lines. Border in mazarine blue with gold edges and cross-hatching forming arches with scroll ends in which are semicircular devices with sprays of gold leaves above. Pl. 111.

924 Gold edge and border lines. Gold wavy leaf and berry border. Broad mazarine blue band with a row of gold devices which appear similiar to arches made from serrated elephant tusks. Various other gold devices also. Pl. 112.

926 All gold decoration. 'Minims pattern'. (Description as received.)

928 Acorns with red. (Description as received.)

934 U299 Gold edge and border lines with green band between. Narrow border of pairs of gold leaves and berries. Black and white print of basket of flowers.

940 Blue edge. Large daisy-like flower in blue picked out in iron-red with other smaller roses and flowers in pink, yellow, and blue with green foliage. Rather crude.

946 (Not confirmed.) Pink band between two narrow yellow bands is decorated with a zigzag white line and darker pink sprays. There is a lower thin pink loop line border. Pl. 113.

947 Magenta edge line and inner line, the pale magenta band between is broken by white cartouches containing yellow flowers and is overdecorated by darker shade zigzag wavy lines. Mainly yellow floral sprays. Pl 114.

953 Iron-red edge and border band. Mauve loops and feathers. Dotted wavy line border. Main spray single magenta rose and green leaves.

966 Band of red star flowers in gold circle on underglaze blue and gold. (Description as received.)

971 Gold edge and border bands. Broad mazarine blue border overdecorated with groups of three white daisies with yellow centres and iron-red inner shading; these alternate with green leaves and gold fronds. Pl. 115.

984 R 1053, 1092, 1159, 1277 Gold edge and border lines. Zigzag line of gold twigs. Polychrome rural print.

1007 Wide blue band between gold lines carrying leafed gold rose sprigs pointing upwards and downwards alternately, under 'Y' chain of gold leaves. Gold rim. (Description as received.)

1011 (Attribution very doubtful.) Shell and scroll moulded edge

outlined in gold. Broad green border decorated with gold foliage and white cartouches each with single rose. Central motif of well-painted spray of three large pink roses.

1016 R Gold edge and border lines. Foliate border in gold and blue. Mazarine blue background over-decorated with medium and large white and orange pansies with central bull's-eye device. Gold leaves and tendrils.

1018 285 Gold edge and border lines. Pairs of wild strawberries alternating with three leaves, all in a reddish-brown colour, connected by a slightly wavy line of gold foliage. Pl. 116.

1033 Blue edge. Pink border band. Sepia rural scene.

1040 Blue edge and border lines. Crude polychrome Chinese-style scene, of a man holding a bird on the end of a stick watched by another person in a window. There is a floral shrub between them. Pl. 117.

1041 Gold edge and border lines. Line of gold leaves angled to each other with interspersed dots. Two lines of blue arrowheads with inter-spersed dots with line of alternating gold leaves between. See p. 82.

1043 Gold edge and border lines. A wavy gold foliate border with occasional small flowers with blue and magenta petals spaced alternately either side of this border.

1045 R Yellow edge. Inner border of pairs of iron-red circles and dots separated by dashes and pairs of dots. Central motif is a yellow scallop shell on a bed of green leaves with red and blue flowers. Sprigs.

1046 Gold edge and border lines. A border of gold stems and berries separated by a mass of iron-red tendrils with central gold leaf.

1052 All gold. A band of zigzag single leaves and dots. Between parallel lines another band of short zigzag lines and dots broken by occasional leaf-like devices.

1053 984, 1092, 1159, 1277 Polychrome rural print within circular gold bordered cartouche.

1054 876, 1163, 2359 Gold edge. Zigzag line of gold hearts between pairs of border lines. Chinese-style scene in mazarine blue, light blue, and orange of an elephant to the left and with buildings and trees all overgilt.

1055 Gold edges and inner gold lines. Border of angled gold leaves with interspersed dots. See p. 82.

1057 Gold edges and lines. A band of mazarine blue vertical and horizontal lines edged with gold forming rectangular cartouches containing iron-red and mazarine blue flowers and foliage with overgilding.

1058 1508, 1551 Large sprays of three large pink roses and one bud and one partly out rose. Yellow leaves with green centres and blue/green leaves. Other small blue sprigs.

1059 Gold edges and border lines. Wavy border of heart-shaped leaves. Mazarine blue rectangles with gold flower-heads joined by light blue chain swags with gold foliage above. Heart-shaped leaf border repeated.

1063 984, 709 Black edge and border lines. Black and white rural prints.

1064 R Brown edge. Central motif is a bouquet of a large pink, large orange, and small yellow flower with green foliage and blue scrolls.

1066 425 Gold edge and border line. Heavily decorated polychrome border and oriental scene known as 'Boy at the Window'. (This is bone china version of patt. 425.)

1070 R Dark brown edges and border lines. Border of small brown leaves. Border of single two-tone green leaves with orange berries and brown stalks between two brown lines. Pl. 118.

1084 R Yellow edge and inner blue line are separated by iron-red circles and pairs of blue circles. Decoration in blue and iron-red shows a house with smoke from top and a foliate spray with two blue flowers.

1085 R Mazarine blue border overgilded. Overall pattern of large flowers in orange, pale, and mazarine blue with mazarine blue stems and green leaves. The whole is overgilded with more flowers and leaves etc.

1092 984, 1053, 1159, 1277 Gold edges and border lines. Pale blue background broken by circular cartouches edged in gold containing polychrome rural prints. Some other gold decoration. Pl. 119.

1100 462, 709 Gold edge and border line. Inner border of pairs of gold leaves alternating with pairs of berries on stalks. Black and white rural prints. Pl. 120.

1109 1147, 1178, 1236, 1277, 1525, U243 Black edge and inner border line. Black and white Adam Buck print of mother and child.

1117 R 1354 Border of two iron-red lines with a wavy line and attached twisted tendrils, also in iron-red, and green leaves between them. Pl. 121.

1119 Gold edge and border lines. Inner gold border of zigzag stems with small leaves. Hand-painted rural scene in a greeny-brown colour. Pl. 122.

1126 1218, 1304, 1318, 1378, 1413 Gold edge and border lines. Two mazarine blue bands, overgilt with leaves and dots, on either side of broad light blue band which is overdecorated with large pink and orange flowers, green/white gilt leaves.

1141 Gold edge and border line. Spray with single harebell and foliage. Other floral sprays all in gold.

1147 1109, 1178, 1236, 1277, 1525 Gold edge. Two thin gold border lines. A border of two rows of gold diamonds. A central narrow gold band of wavy sprigs. Black and white Adam Buck print.

1152 Gold edge and border lines. Border of pairs of green leaves connected by pairs of orange swags which have gold pendants at their junctions. Pl. 123.

1153 R 1313 Gold edge and border line. Overall Japan-style plant with mazarine blue stem and orange flowers, other white flowers and leaves in two tones of green. Overgilt. Gold zigzag border of small leaves. Pl. 124.

1157 Black edge. Painted sprays. (Description as received.)

1159 984, 1053, 1092, 1277 Gold edge and border lines. Broad mazarine blue band overdecorated with gold vines and oval cartouches of polychrome fruit on a white background. Central polychrome rural print.

1160 Gold edge and border lines. Gold zigzag border of leaves. Broad mazarine blue band decorated with face-on single white flowers separated by two angled white flowers with orange dots. Green leaves. Pl. 125.

1161 Gold edge. A border of large three-point mazarine blue leaves with a single leaf and acorns between. Below are groups of three five-petalled pink flowers with orange centres. All heavily overgilt.

1162 Gold edge and border lines. Broad mazarine blue band is overdecorated with gold and white diamonds with a mazarine blue cross and gold petals. Between is gold foliage and cherry swags. Pl. 126.

1163 2358, 2359 Gold edge. Chinese-style scene in light blue, mazarine blue, and orange showing man crossing bridge over river with boat. Buildings left and right. Central large tree. Man in foreground. Heavily gilt. Col. Pl. I, Pl. 127.

1169 Blue edge and band. Border of large single flowers in yellow and brown connected by sparse brown and green foliage. Pl. 128.

1172 Polychrome oriental scene of three people, and sometimes a child, in front of a paling fence and a small simple summer-house.

1173 R Iron-red band with scrolls attached. Main decoration consists of a vase of flowers in various colours and a blue lighted candle. Other orange flowers. Pl. 129.

1178 1109, 1147, 1236, 1277, 1525 Gold edge. Black and white Adam Buck mother and child prints.

1180 Blue edge and border lines. Broad light magenta band overlaid with darker leaf sprigs separated by single dots. Central polychrome bouquet of flowers including pink rose. Several polychrome sprigs.

1181 Yellow edge and border lines. Crudely-painted single orange flowers with leaves in green and yellowy green. Pl. 130.

1214 Gold edge and border lines. Border of alternate pairs of gold leaves and berries. Chinese-style scene in mazarine, mid and light blue,

and orange. Buildings, fence, large tiger. Bush with bird. Overgilt. Pl. 131.

1218 1126, 1304, 1318, 1378, 1413 Gold edge and border lines. Two mazarine blue borders overgilt with angled 'f's. Broad light blue border between with large single alternate pale pink and orange flowers with green leaves. Pl. 132.

1219 R Gold edge and border lines. Mazarine blue border overgilt with 'f's. Overall decoration of single mazarine blue flowers and stalks, orange flowers, green leaves, yellow fruits, and gold tendrils. Pl. 133.

1221 Gold-edged wavy line border. Overall mazarine blue background with one very large orange-centred white flower, a pair of white and two different mauve flowers, green leaves, and overgilding.

1230 Green edge. Central bouquet of a rose, a yellow and a blue flower with two-tone green foliage and smaller flowers. A few similar smaller sprays at edges. Pl. 134.

1235 Black edge. Two different sorts of large orange flowers are connected by a continuous stem with smaller flowers, with large green leaves and skeletal sprays of orange leaves. Naive painting.

1236 1109, 1147, 1178, 1277, 1525 Gold edge and border line. Polychrome Adam Buck print of children playing.

1238 (Not confirmed.) Sprays resembling three radishes alternating with seaweed in puce, iron-red, and green.

1240 Wide border of a pink rose on a brown stem with green leaves and some small yellow flowers with emerald green leaves.

1244 Blue edge and border line. Large main spray has two yellow-centred magenta flowers and two blue flowers with green and black leaves. Lesser sprays have a blue and a magenta flower or both in blue. Pl. 135.

1252 Gold edge and border line. A zigzag gold line with dots above and below. A wide gold band arched on the underside with loops at ends and large foliate pendants. Pl. 136.

1255 (Not confirmed.) Pale blue border, berries, and foliage, gilt highlights.

1263 Gold edge and border line. A zigzag gold border line of hearts. Between two gold lines a broad border of two mazarine blue leaves, an orange, mazarine blue, and green flower and an orange bud, all overgilt. Pl. 137.

1266 Gold edge and line. Gold zigzag border of three leaf twigs and dots. Broad mazarine blue band overdecorated with large white pansy, red and white tulip, other flowers, green leaves, and foliate overgilding. Pl. 138.

1267 Gold-edged broad mazarine blue border with gold decoration comprised of diamonds, scrolls with leaf appendages, and laurel leaves.

1270 829, 1272, 1415 Mazarine blue and gold border band. Medium blue ground. Pairs of large strawberries with large white flowers and single large three-pointed green leaves. Gold tendrils.

1272 829, 1270, 1415 Mazarine blue and gold border band. Medium blue ground. Pairs of large strawberries with large white flowers and single large three-pointed green leaves. Gold tendrils.

1277 1109, 1147, 1178, 1236, 1525 Gold edge and border lines. Broad mazarine blue band overdecorated with gold vines and oval cartouches of polychrome fruit on white background. Central polychrome Adam Buck print of mother and child. Pl. 139.

1279 Gold edge and border lines between which are single mazarine blue flowers with orange centres interspersed with gilt foliage, tendrils and buds. Pl. 140.

1296 R Blue edge, brown border, polychrome swags with pink rose at bottom.

1304 1126, 1218, 1318, 1378, 1413 Gold edge and border lines. Two mazarine blue bands overgilt by zigzag lines and hearts bordering a broad light blue band decorated with a triple orange harebell, pink edged white flower, green leaves.

1311 R Black edge and border lines. Black-edged band of single yellow-centred magenta flowers with dark green leaves almost completely filling space between lines. Rather dark decoration. Pl. 141.

1313 1153, U107, U209 Gold edge and border lines. Zigzag of gold hearts. Japan-style plant with mazarine blue stem and pale pink flowers of various shapes. Green oak leaves. All overgilt. Pl. 142.

1318 1126, 1218, 1304, 1378, 1413 Gold edge and border lines. Single mazarine blue band overgilt with hearts and dots. Broad pale blue band with five-pointed pale pink flowers with gold and magenta centres. White and gold foliage.

1325 Gold edge and border lines. Chinese-style scene in mazarine blue, orange, magenta, and green. Main feature is a large magenta stepped bridge with an orange figure, buildings, and shrubbery. All is overgilt. Pl. 143.

1327 Gold edge and border line between which is a zigzag line with gold hearts and dots. A broad mazarine blue and gold seaweed border broken by single large faded pink flowers. Pl. 144.

1332 Gold edge. The mazarine blue border, undulating on the lower side and overgilt with scrolls, is broken by gold-edged orange devices and single white leaves. Under are single orange and green flowers.

1344 (Possibly 1544, unclear no.) Gold edges and border lines. Zigzag line of gold hearts. Broad pale green band overdecorated with large pink rose, pink flower, orange-edged flowers, two-tone green leaves, other blue and gold foliage. Pl. 145.

1354 1117 Brown edge. The brown border consists of a wavy line with short tendrils attached both sides and with interspersed single blobs. (Attribution not confirmed.)

1357 Gold edge and border lines. Polychrome fruit still life. Peaches, plums, cherries, leaves, etc. Pl. 146.

1359 R Blue edge and border line with broad border of sparsely-decorated roses, daisies, etc. in various colours.

1361 1373, 1542, U122, U126 Mazarine blue and gilt border band. Overall decoration of coloured peony branches with mazarine blue and gilt foliage and tendrils.

1363 R Blue edge band. Pale magenta border edged with darker dots and decorated with darker groups of three leaves and a dot. Main spray features a large and a small two-tone magenta flower and green leaves. Pl. 147.

1371 1453, 1485, 1498, 1571, 1830 Blue edge and border. Continuous border of large pink flowers, medium yellow flowers, and small iron-red flowers joined by foliage with veined green leaves and plain blue and green leaves.

1373 Gold edge and border lines. Mazarine blue border band overgilt with a line of wishbone devices. A pale blue background is decorated with a mazarine blue bush and with brown, yellow, and magenta flowers. Gilded.

1378 R 1126, 1218, 1304, 1318, 1413 Gold edges and border lines. Mazarine blue bands overgilt with leaves and dotted ring between which is a blue band with large pink roses, smaller orange and yellow flowers with green and gilt foliage. Pl. 148.

1385 Yellow bands with scale pink areas which are edged in blue with central blue diamonds and orange and blue oriental-style floral sprays between. Other decoration is an orange and blue pagoda.

1397 R Gold edge. Large polychrome floral bouquet, the main large flowers being a pink rose, a mauve tulip, and an iron-red pansy. There are also two small sprays.

1398 Gold edge and border lines. Mazarine blue rectangular panels with central iron-red roundels. Naively painted floral panels in iron-red, mazarine blue, and green. Mazarine blue looped lower border. Overgilt.

1399 R Brown edge and border line. Border consists of tiny brown floral sprays sprouting from a close band of small two-tone green leaves in arrowhead formation.

1400 Gold edge and border line between which is a floral band containing pink rose, mauve tulip with yellow centre, and other lesser flowers in yellow, iron red and blue with multi-tone green leaves. Pl. 149.

1401 R Gold edge and border line with between a broad border of single Catherine wheel like flowers in pink

and yellow joined by wavy line of magenta sprigs, small buds, green leaves, and small blue flowers.

1403 Gold edge and border lines between which is a row of individual pink flowers seen from beneath alternating with single green leaves and joined by thin loops of stems.

1409 Gold edge and border lines. Band of single large formalized mauve flowers fading to white with yellow centres separated by blue-green leaves and small individual iron-red and blue flowers. Pl. 150.

1411 R Gold edge. Mazarine blue border is loop shaped on lower side with thin lines to centre gold line and overdecoration of single blooms and gold scrolls. Rest: iron-red flowers, green leaves, blue stems. Pl. 151.

1413 1126, 1218, 1304, 1318, 1378 Gold edge and borders. Mazarine blue bands, overgilt with wavy line of foliage, either side of broad blue band decorated with pink peonies and green foliage. Pl. 152.

1415 829, 1270 Gold edges and border lines. Mazarine blue border overgilt with dashes. Pale blue background with pairs of strawberries separated by single white flower with green leaves and gold tendrils etc. Pl. 153.

1421 R Gold edge and border line with broad mazarine blue band between overdecorated with large single two-tone pink flowers with yellow centres and black dots, green leaves and gold foliage. Pl. 154.

1426 Gold edge and border lines. A broad floral border, three pink flowers followed by a yellow flower followed by four more pink flowers all interspersed with green leaves and repeated throughout border. Pl. 155.

1428 R Gold edge. Separated magenta ribbon swags with five-petalled black flower each end and elderberry tendrils in blue one end and magenta the other with other decoration. Polychrome sprigs.

1434 R Blue edge and border line. Border of large iron-red flowers with black and yellow centres interspersed with mauve or blue yellow-centred flowers and two-tone green foliage.

1435 R Brown edge. Brown large stemmed bush with blobs of iron-red and two-tone green as flowers and foliage. Brown rock with floral spray in yellow, mauve, and blue growing from it.

1442 R 1444, U266 Orange edge and border lines (also seen in yellow). Central bouquet of magenta, iron-red, yellow, and blue flowers with two-tone green foliage. Smaller sprays of various flowers. Crude and simple.

1444 R 1442, U266 Mid blue edge and border lines (also seen in yellow). Central bouquet of magenta, iron-red, yellow, and blue flowers with two-tone green foliage. Smaller sprays of various flowers. Crude and simple. Pl. 156.

1445 R Pink edge, inner and outer border lines. Border of well-spaced pink roses each with green foliage.

1450 Gold dentil edge. Broad gold undulating foliate border band with alternate solid and veined leaves and single emerald green flowers. Under is a wavy gold line and a lower gold line of connected leaves. Pl. 157.

1453 R 1371, 1485, 1498, 1571, 1830 Gold edges and borders. Gold zigzag line of hearts. Border of large pink flowers, medium yellow flowers, and small iron-red flowers joined by foliage with veined green leaves and plain two-tone leaves. Col. Pl. I, Pl. 158.

1458 Gold edges and border lines. Mazarine blue border gilt with leaves and dots in arrow shape. Background light blue with large pink flower, outer edge is in two-tone mauve with dots. Green and gold foliage.

1474 R Gold edge and border lines. Broad mazarine blue border zigzag bottom with row of pink flowers at top interspersed with curly-edged white cartouches at bottom containing gold sprays. Overall gilding. Pl. 159.

1477 Gold edge and border lines. Main colour of background is blue, white flower moulded border. Broken inner orange border with white foliage. Remainder has pink and white flowers etc. Mazarine blue centre band.

1478 1706, U271 Gold edge. Blue border with flower moulding. Centre decoration of a polychrome rural scene. Alternatives are fruit, flowers, or a basket of fruit.

1480 R 1506 Gold edge and border lines. Pink background with white flower moulded border. Gold foliate inner border broken by gold-edged oval cartouches with polychrome sprigs. Central rose and floral bouquet.

1485 1371, 1453, 1498, 1571, 1830 Gold edge and border. Continuous border of large pink flowers, medium yellow flowers, and small iron-red flowers joined by foliage with veined green leaves and plain blue and green leaves.

1496 R Gold edge. Centre bottom is a shell-like device in iron-red and blue from which sprout two mauve flowers, three orange tulips, orange and yellow daisy with other lesser flowers and green foliage. Sprays.

1498 R 1371, 1453, 1485, 1571, 1380 Brown edge and borders. Continuous border of large pink flowers, medium yellow flowers, and small iron-red flowers joined by foliage with veined green leaves and plain blue and green leaves.

1506 R 1480 Green background, white moulded flowers, band of polychrome floral sprays. Gold edges.

1507 Gold edge, puce-coloured rural print.

1508 R 1058, 1551 Gold edge. Large sprays of three large pink roses and one bud and one partly out rose. Leaves are mainly yellow with green centres and a few are blue green. There are some small sprays. Pl. 160.

1511 R 1513 A mainly mauve bird on a branch with mauve flowers and leaves, orange flower and buds, green and blue/green leaves, and two moths.

1513 1511 (Unconfirmed.) A mainly mauve bird on a branch with mauve flowers and leaves, orange flower and buds, green and blue/green leaves, and a butterfly.

1525 1109, 1147, 1178, 1236, 1277 Gold edge and border lines. Polychrome Adam Buck print of mother and child.

1535 R Gold edges and borders. Border of small heart-shaped leaves on zigzag straight lines. Main decoration: angled gold fronds interspersed with gold ovals and two dots. Pl. 161.

1541 U168 Mazarine blue border over gilt with small leaves. Chinese-style picture of mazarine blue and orange building in centre. Tree right. Bridge bottom left. Iron-red rocks foreground and left. Overall gilding.

1542 Gold edge and border lines. Mazarine blue overgilt stem and large leaves with large orange flowers, a few smaller orange flowers, small green leaves, and gold tendrils.

1543 R Mazarine blue and gold. Floral decoration. (Description as received.)

1544 See 1344.

1547 R A spray of small green leaves with small blue and red flowers.

1551 R 1058, 1508 Gold edge. Sprays of pink roses, three large, one half open and one bud, yellow leaves with green centres, and blue/green leaves. Other small blue sprigs.

1553 R 1560 Gold edge and border line. Central bouquet of large magenta flower, large two-tone orange flower, three mauve and two blue flowers, and two-tone green foliage.

1554 R 1669 Gold edges. Monochrome green floral sprays. Pl. 162.

1560 1553 Magenta edge and border lines. Central bouquet of large magenta flower, large two-tone orange flower, three mauve and two blue flowers, and two-tone green foliage.

1563 R Gold edges and borders. Inner border of heart-shaped leaves on zigzag stalks with dots. All gold floral sprays with buds and flower centres picked out in orange. One orange fern leaf.

1571 R 1371, 1453, 1485, 1498, 1830 Continuous border of large pink flowers, medium yellow flowers, and small iron-red flowers joined by foliage with veined green leaves and plain blue and green leaves. Pl. 163.

1575 Gold edges. Broad border of orange and iron-red flowers with blue/green leaves and mazarine blue rock split up by cartouches in mazarine blue with central white diamond overdecorated with gold leaves. Pl. 164.

1597 Gold rim. Large floral sprays comprised of two large pink rose-like flowers, one bud, and three small orange flowers. Blue and green foliage.

1600 1831 Gold edge. Wide floral border comprising large pink petal flowers with yellow centres, pink buds, pairs of smaller blue and white flowers, large green leaves, small blue and green leaves, and brown stems. Pl. 165.

1610 Gold edges and border lines. Edge border of zigzag stems with three small leaves. Broad border of single fern leaves alternating with a row of four circles all on the diagonal. All in gold. Pl. 166.

1613 R Single bird, mainly mauve, with yellow breast sitting with outspread wings on brown branch which has large flowers in mauve, iron-red, and pink with green, blue, and yellow foliage.

1614 R Two birds coloured blue, iron-red, and yellow sitting on branches of a brown tree stump with green leaves and pink flowers. Col. Pl. I.

1618 Three large crudely-painted oak leaves in green and blue, brown twigs with yellow and green acorns. Pl. 167.

1621 R Brown border line. Broad border of linked green foliage with pairs of blue leaves, three parallel orange buds, small orange flowers, and single flowers with seven black dots.

1623 R Brown edge. Broad border of continuous magenta elderberry stalk with a profusion of small black berries. A few magenta sprigs also.

1634 (Unconfirmed.) Clusters of sprigs with blue flowers and green leaves separated by short lines of similar sprigs.

1641 Gold edges and wavy line sprig borders between gold lines. Main background is mazarine blue with edge-on pink flower. Lower panels of green foliage, orange flowers with mazarine blue. Overgilt. Pl. 168.

1653 Gold edge, border lines, and zigzag leaf spray border. Broad mud-green band overdecorated with large single pink roses, big magenta flowers, small blue and orange flowers with two-tone green leaves. Pl. 169.

1659 Gold edge. Gold central spray and sprigs. Large floral sprays in pink, iron-red, blue, and yellow with leaves in green and yellow. Pl. 170.

1669 R 1554 Monochrome green floral sprays.

1677 Various delicate pink flowers with large blue leaves, smaller green leaves, and some overgilding.

1680 Gold edge and border lines. A border of blue blobs connected by gold foliage. Overall pattern of gilt dark blue leaves and gold tendrils. Main flower with pink petals, yellow centre, and large mauve dots.

1681 Gold edges. Exotic long-tailed bird on fence, another swooping.

Exotic tree. Main colours are mazarine blue and orange with much overgilding.

1695 Gold edges and border lines. Broad fawn band with row of large single mauve flowers with green leaves overpainted. Iron-red pointed trefoils and gilt foliage. Col. Pl. I.

1696 Gold edges and border lines. Broad fawn border with line of single pink dog roses, orange buds, and gilt foliage. Pl. 171.

1699 Gold edges and border lines. Broad band of single pink roses, blue daisies, and orange daisies connected by green foliage.

1700 Gold edges and bands. Broad band of single large flowers. The round pink flower has many black dots, the yellow and brown is seen from the back and side. Blue/green oak leaves, green foliage, blue flowers. Pl. 172.

1706 1478, 1707 Blue border bird moulded. Inner mazarine blue and gilt border. Centre decoration: polychrome fruit with gilt fern leaves. Pl. 173.

1707 1706 Overall mid blue background with bird moulded border. Gold rim. Two mazarine blue bands overgilt with dashes with single large pink roses and buds separated by green leaves. All overgilt. Pl. 174.

1710 Gold edges and border lines. Mazarine blue edge band overgilt with a wavy tendril. Pale blue background. Pink rose cartouches. Inner gold and white leaf device. Pl. 175.

1725 (Not confirmed.) Bat-printed farmyard scenes, gilt highlights and border.

1742 1749 (Note alternatives.) Gold or green border and line. Plain (bird or flower moulded) border. Bunches of flowers with a pink rose, mauve, iron-red, and little blue flowers. Green leaves. Pl. 176.

1749 1742 (Patt. no. unverified.) Green edge and black inner border line. Flower moulded border. Bunches of flowers with a pink rose, mauve, iron-red, and little blue flowers. Green leaves. (Could be misnumbered 1742 variation.)

1756 Gold edge and border lines. Mazarine blue border is overdecorated with pink-edged white daisies, iron-red and white peonies, pairs of gold and white oak and other leaves, and overall small gold leaf sprays. Pl. 177.

1762 (Refers to gilding only.) Blue willow pattern with band of up/down alternating grenades. Pl. 178.

1770 Green edge and border line bird moulded. Central large bouquet of pink rose, mauve, dark orange, and yellow flowers with green foliage. Other small sprays each with flowers in different colours. Pl. 179.

1772 Hand-coloured transfer-printed sprays of a variety of flowers in magenta, blue, iron-red, and yellow with two-tone yellow and green leaves. Pl. 180.

1810 (Not confirmed.) Gold 'Warburtons Patent' print of children under a tree.

1819 Broad band of single large rosebuds connected by yellow-centred forget-me-nots and green foliage. Pl. 181.

1820 Blue edge and border lines. Band of single pink roses, blue flowers, and iron-red flowers alternating and connected by a line of green foliage. Pl. 182.

1822 R Gold edge and border line. Broad band comprising large single pink roses, brown twigs with small yellow flowers, green leaves, and blue/green catkins. Pl. 183.

1830 R 1371, 1453, 1485, 1498, 1571 Gold edge and border lines. Broad band of single pink flowers with black dots, smaller yellow and mauve flower, and pink bud connected by two-tone green foliage. Pl. 184.

1831 1600 A border of single large mainly pink flowers separated by pairs of blue flowers and green leaves and connected by a tendril.

1856 U172 (Refers to gilding.) Gold edge and border lines. Light blue reversed Willow Pattern-type scene with two persons on the bridge and no doves. A broad overgilding band of tendrils, sprigs, and large half solid gold leaves.

1857 Gold edge and border lines. Gold foliate inner border. Broad fawn band, arched at bottom, is overdecorated with round green cartouches containing a pink and white flower. Covered in gold foliage. Pl. 185.

1865 1915 Border and inner band in mazarine blue overgilt. Between bands a row of single pink roses each with five green leaves and fine gilt connecting foliage.

1872 Gold edge and border lines. Sage green ground and bird moulded border. Inner mazarine blue borders overgilt. Overdecoration of large stylized pink and small magenta flowers. Foliate gilding.

1874 U246 Blue border bird moulded. Two inner bands of gilt mazarine blue, between is a line of large well-painted pink roses with green leaves and gold tendrils on white. A similar rose decorates centre.

1897 1930, 1939, 2018, 2171, 2188 Edge lines. Basket weave moulding. Cartouches contain an iron-red daisy in centre with a two-tone pink rose one side and a shaded white daisy the other. Some of the green leaves are shaded.

1915 1865 Gold edge and border. Band of single pink roses each with five green leaves and connected spray with five yellow buds.

1927 1944, 1945 Gold edge and border lines. Mazarine blue band overgilt. Basket-weave border. Car-

touches contain simple floral decoration in light blue, mazarine blue, iron-red and green with overgilding. Pl. 186.

1929 Basket weave moulding. Cartouche contains two-tone blue floral spray. A few similar sprigs on border. (Possibly unfinished decoration.)

1930 1897, 1939, 2018, 2188 Basket-weave moulding. Iron-red edge band. Floral cartouches. Central flower is magenta, upper one is yellow, left one is khaki and yellow, others are small in blue and orange. Green and yellow leaves.

1934 Gold edge and border line. Border of single gold harebells separated by pairs of fern leaves. Hand-painted polychrome rural scenes.

1935 Gold edge and border line between which is a zigzag line with gold hearts and dots. Polychrome rural prints. Pl. 187.

1939 1897, 1930, 2018, 2171, 2188 Basket-weave moulding. Cartouches of bunches of flowers. The centre one is magenta, upper one is yellow, left one is khaki and yellow, others are small in blue and orange. Green and yellow leaves. Pl. 188.

1944 1927, 1945 Basket-weave or plain border. Overgilt mazarine blue bands. Gold scrolled edge cartouches contain a single yellow tulip or other floral sprays. Central ring contains pink, blue, and orange flowers. Pl. 189.

1945 1927, 1944 Basket-weave border, mazarine blue and gilt bands. Cartouches of polychrome floral sprays. Inner border broken by vertical mazarine blue and gilt bands with polychrome floral sprays between.

1956 Gold edge and border line. Border band of individual pink roses, orange marigolds, blue cornflowers, etc. and green foliage. Polychrome rural scene. Pl. 190.

1976 Gold edges and border lines. Mazarine blue band overdecorated with gold acorns and oak leaves.

1978 Gold edge and border line. Zigzag border of narrow gold leaves and dots. Overall decoration of large pink rose, four-petal yellow flower with two blue tufts. Two buds, green leaves, and smaller flowers. Pl. 191.

1980 Gold edges and border lines. All gold pattern of single large flowers joined by a scroll of foliage with single harebell and fern-like leaves. Pl. 192.

1983 Gold edge and border lines. Narrow wavy band of thin single leaves with a dot between. Broad complex foliate band with individual large leaves predominating. All in gold. Pl. 193.

2008 Gold edge and border lines. Broad pale blue band overdecorated with orange flowers and leaf scrollwork in gold. Pl. 194.

2011 Basket-weave moulded border with plain cartouches containing one or two pink roses with green leaves. Inner border of similar single pink roses interspersed with green leaves.

2018 1897, 1930, 1939, 2171, 2188 Basket-weave border, cartouches contain a pink rose with other coloured flowers and two-tone leaves. Large central spray consists of pink rose, yellow flower, white flower, small flowers, and blue/green foliage. Pl. 195.

2022 (Not confirmed.) Mazarine blue and gilt deep undulating border over well painted sprigs.

2050 2063, 2155 Basket-weave border in blue and green. The white background cartouches contain pink roses, magenta, blue, yellow, and mauve flowers, green leaves. Central bouquet similar. Gold borders and edges.

2054 Gold edge. Broad mazarine blue border is broken by oval cartouches each containing different polychrome floral sprays. Border is heavily overgilded with leaves and edged with scrolls. Pl. 196.

2058 Gilding, blue ground, and roses. (Description as received.)

2063 2050, 2155 Blue and green basket-weave border, white background cartouches contain fruit and leaves. Central bouquet of several kinds of fruit and berries with green and tan leaves. Borders and edges gilded.

2082 Gold edge and border lines. Basket-weave moulded body. The individual printed flowers within the cartouches are overdecorated with enamels.

2094 A magenta rose and a yellow-centred orange flower close together and surrounded by closely-packed two-tone green leaves and brown tendrils forming an almost rectangular spray. Pl. 197.

2098 Gold edge lines. Undulating border of gold leaves and dark blue flowers. Broad mazarine blue band upon which is a broad gold tube device with encircling rings and leaves. A border of gold trident devices.

2102 Unclear no. possibly 2162/2702. Gold edge and border lines. Zigzag border of gold three-leaf twigs and dots. Mazarine blue bands overgilded with foliate tendril. Main decoration: pairs of pink roses separated by coloured bird. Pl. 198.

2103 2268 Overall white basket-weave. Cartouches contain pink rose, green buds, and a profusion of gold fern-like leaves. Inner wavy border of gold stem of leaves with gold line to either side. Pl. 199.

2120 Broad fawn border with gold edges overdecorated with black leaf sprays. Black and white spray in centre consists of one large rose, rosebuds, and foliage. Pl. 200.

2128 Main colour pale blue with octagonal white cartouches which contain multicoloured floral bouquets. Pale blue part is over-decorated with single mazarine blue

star-bursts, gold edges, and gold scroll work.

2141 (Unconfirmed.) Brightly-painted flowers.

2155 2050, 2063 Broad mid blue border with wide gold decorative edges, inner gold line, and inner border of crossing wavy gold lines. Central bouquet of pink roses, blue, mauve, and orange flowers with green leaves.

2162 See 2102.

2171 1897, 1930, 1939, 2018, 2188 Bird moulding. Green edge lines. Large central bouquet comprising large pink rose, yellow pansy, small blue and orange flowers with yellow centres, green foliage. Handle picked out in magenta.

2172 Basket-weave moulding. Hand-coloured transfer-printed floral decoration in magenta, iron-red, and blue/green. Main cartouche contains a square and a round jardinière with flowers. Pl. 201.

2179 Gold edge and bands. Gold foliate border. Mazarine blue overgilt edge bands. Overall decoration of large pink rose, puce-edged yellow, formalized blue, orange-centred white and other flowers. Gilding. Pl. 202.

2180 Gold border lines. Mazarine blue background heavily overgilt with scrolls, swags, foliage, and trumpet device. The polychrome floral cartouches feature a large pink-edged yellow tulip.

2181 (Not confirmed.) Polychrome floral sprays between mazarine blue and gilt panels.

2183 Swags of small blue flowers and green leaves joined by large pink roses with green leaves and brown twiglets. Pl. 203.

2184 Moulded floral sprays. Hand-painted blue and white scene of a tall vase of flowers, a broad squat vase of flowers, and a box-like object. Pl. 204.

2188 1897, 1930, 1939, 2018, 2171 Bird moulded border edged with green lines. Large central bouquet comprising large pink rose, yellow pansy, small blue and orange flowers with yellow centres and green foliage.

2226 Gold lines. Moulded floral sprays separated by differing polychrome floral sprays. Main spray of blue harebells, pink roses and buds, shaded iron-red and a white daisy, florets, and green leaves. Pl.205.

2229 Gold edge. White moulded floral spray interspersed with gold leaves on light blue band. Inner arched gold band. Inner arched gold band. Central polychrome painted rural scene which includes people. Pl. 206.

2239 Bird moulded border edged with brown lines. Central bouquet of pink, mauve, and yellow flowers, also buds. Two-tone green and turquoise foliage. Pl.207.

2240 Gold edge. White moulded floral spray, interspersed with polychrome sprigs, on pale blue band. Broad gold inner border. Central polychrome fruit.

2258 A border of a pair of overlapping pink daisies alternating with an iron-red flower and connected by green foliage with two blue florets. The main flowers have yellow centres.

2268 2103 Border of a wavy stem of gold leaves. Overall white basket weave. Cartouches contain a pink rose, green buds, and a few gold fern-like leaves. (Marked 'Sevres'.)

2274 Gold edges and lines. Gold and blue foliate border band. The mazarine blue band is scrolled on the underside and overgilded with scrolls and foliage. Sprays of blue harebells, pink roses, etc. on the white.

2275 White background, pale blue cartouches with single white flower and mazarine blue borders. Pink flowers and green foliage on main body. Mazarine blue border with gold swags and edges. Overall gilding. Pl. 208.

2283 Gold edge and border lines. Gold hatched border band arched on lower side with pendant florets and spaced single pink roses. Main spray of a blue delphinium, yellow and red flower with green foliage. Pl. 209.

2299 Basket-weave moulding. Edge line, arched border with connecting trident devices and ovals under, all in gold. The cartouches contain various floral sprays with pink roses and other flowers in blue and red etc.

2343 Brown line edges to plain border. Inner border of single pink roses, yellow, blue, and brown flowers interspersed with green leaves.

2350 Basket-weave border with brown edge line and single flower spray in cartouches. Central motif of three mauve leaves and orange flower with mauve and orange buds. Remainder is brown twigs and green leaves. Pl. 210.

2358 2359, 1163 Mazarine blue border to scene containing arch to right, temple left rear, central tree, man, woman, and dog foreground. Main colours are mazarine blue, pale blue, and orange. Gilded. Pl. 211.

2359 1163, 2358 Rural scene, main colours orange, pale blue, and mazarine blue. Ruin to left, tree to right in mazarine blue with gold leaves. Two orange deer in foreground. Highly gilded overall.

2369 Bird moulded border with green edges within which are bouquets of pink, blue, orange, and yellow flowers with green leaves. There are also several small sprays dotted about. Pl. 212.

2371 Gold edge. White moulded floral spray. Yellow inner line. Large floral spray features a large pink rose, four iron-red daisies, several flowers in other colours including blue.

2383 Basket-weave border, cartouches contain birds and foliage. Centre contains bird flying to nest in floral bush. Colours not known. (Also gilded.) Pl. 213.

2384 Gold edges and leafy border band. Mazarine blue border, sepentine on lower edge is heavily overgilded with stylized white daisy and fronds etc. Well-painted floral sprays with variety of flowers.

2387 (Unconfirmed.) Mazarine blue ground overdecorated with greenish roses with white and gold leaves. Gold tracery.

2449 Gold edge and border lines. Pink basket-weave border band. Cartouches contain simple floral decoration. Large polychrome floral spray on body. Line of gold leaves. Pl. 214.

2450 Gold edge and border lines. White moulded floral sprays. Overall fawn background is broken by a white cross containing a polychrome floral spray in each arm and a central rose. Some overgilding.

2452 Gold edge and border lines. White moulded floral sprays on mazarine blue border separated by gold grape and vine leaf motif. The floral spray includes a large puce tulip, a pink rose, and other flowers. Pl. 215.

2472 Broad floral border consists of large blue daisies with iron-red centres connected by a stem of three brown and green leaves, three red berries, and a bud.

2483 (Not confirmed.) Blue and white pagoda pattern with (unspecified) gilding.

2488 U172 has 'R' mark. Gold edge

and border lines. Light blue reversed willow pattern type scene with two persons on the bridge and no doves outlined in gold. (Patt. no. refers to gilding.) Pl. 216.

2493 Blue edge. A simple floral spray comprised of a stem with a single large iron-red petalled flower with yellow base, a pink pansy and leaves in two tones of green. Pl. 217.

2506 (Attribution not confirmed.) Gold edge and border lines. Undulating gold foliate band. Gold floral sprays pendant from inner gold line.

2576 Large pink roses, with gilt highlights.

2603 Broad dark blue band, alternate white and pink roses, green and gold leaves with gold leafy sprays between.

2623 2679 Gold edge and border lines. White moulded floral sprays on mazarine blue border. Heavy overgilding. Central polychrome Dr Syntax scene.

2679 2623 Gold edge and border lines. White moulded floral sprays on mazarine blue border separated by octagonal cartouches of floral sprigs. Heavy overgilding. Central polychrome Dr Syntax scene. Pl. 218.

2702 See 2102.

2733 (Refers to gilding.) Gold edge, gold zigzag border of leaves and dots. Broad gold band of a large rose, pairs of thistles and large leaves all

superimposed over a blue and white printed scene.

2737 Attribution not confirmed. Mazarine blue and gilt border band, inner gilt decorative border. Central large spray of finely-painted flowers. Pl. 219.

2769 U249 Ribbon-handled and floral spray moulded border. All white with polychrome floral sprays between mouldings. Main spray consists of a large rose and another flower.

2802 Gold edge and border lines the inner one is corrugated on one side. An inner band of gold grenades connected by loops with dots and sprigs. Polychrome floral sprays. Heavy gilding with scrolls and foliage.

2804 Gold edge band. Undulating gold foliate border. Gold border of scrolls, tongues of flame, dots, and foliage. Groups of a pink rose, a magenta flower, and a yellow-centred blue flower. Pl. 220.

2825 (Not verified.) Gold edge. Bird moulding. Main spray of a pink rose, a yellow flower, and other flowerlets. Two smaller sprays, one with two roses and a bud, the other with a blue flower and two buds. Blue/green leaves. Pl. 221.

2844 Floral spray moulded border interspersed with polychrome floral sprays. Main spray comprises a pink rose, a magenta flower, and a blue-edged flower fading to white with orange centre. Well painted.

2881 Gold edge line. Border of three rows of gold leaves. Broad gold border band with scrolled edges to white cartouches each containing a polychrome floral spray. A dentil-edged gold line beneath. Pl. 222.

2899 Gold border lines. Inner gold border is dentate on the lower edge with trefoils on the points. A long stemmed magenta bloom sprouts from a pink rose, orange bloom, and a grey-edged white bloom group.

2901 Gold edge. Groups of four or five pink roses with green leaves in a line above a pair of thistles and separated by a four-leaf fern device sprouting from cross-hatched devices all in gold. Col. Pl. O, Pl. 223.

2930 Shell moulding. Gold edges to broad mazarine border overgilded with scrollwork. The cartouches and main spray are well-painted in polychrome, a two-tone tulip being the predominant feature. Pl. 224.

2932 3057 Shell and scroll moulded edge outlined in gold. Broad pale blue border heavily overgilt with bell-shaped foliate devices. Central well-painted spray of large pink rose and other flowers. Col. Pl. P.

3017 Gold edge and border lines. Polychrome floral cartouches separated by overgilt mazarine blue sections with central cream and gold oval devices. Pl. 225.

3032 Shell moulding. Broken edge band in mazarine blue with trellis gilding. Groups of four pink roses. Central polychrome painted rural scene surrounded by a mazarine blue and gilt band. Pl. 226.

3035 Shell and scroll moulded edge. Well-painted large floral spray with yellow and red tulip, pink rose, other lesser flowers in blue, orange, and yellow with green leaves. Another lesser spray. Pl. 227.

3048 Chinoiserie-style bush with large pink flowers and green leaves growing from blue rock, two small figures in brown and pink with coolie hats to left and right. Lower background is pale blue. Pl. 228.

3050 Gold edge lines. Border of gold scrolls and leaves. Broad mazarine blue band with scrolled edged polychrome floral cartouches edged in gold. The upper gold edge band is trellis, the lower plain. Pl. 229.

3057 2932 Shell and scroll moulded edge outlined in gold. Broad maroon border. Gold inner border of 'quaver'-shaped devices and leaves. Main motif of well-painted pink rose and other flowers in various colours. Pl. 230.

3074 Gold edge lines. Oriental-style overgilt decoration, mainly in mazarine blue and iron-red, consists of a corner of a fence on a mound, a small blue vase of large flowers. Various other flowers.

3113 Groups of three flowers and foliage, two of the flowers touch one above the other and the third is apart to the left. A few sprigs. All decoration in magenta.

3203 (Unconfirmed attribution.) Iron-red, magenta, blue, and green floral edge band. A similarly coloured oriental scene comprising figures, a fence, and a 'kiosk'-type building.

3224 Broad floral border consists of single large magenta roses with green leaves connected by a stem of pairs of buds and tendril-enclosed small blue flowers.

3278 Gold edge and border bands. Gilt scroll-edged mazarine blue border overdecorated with blue diamonds and ovals, fawn rings, and gold scrollwork. Below are small polychrome rural scenes. Pl. 231.

3306 3639, 3669 seem identical. Gold edge and border lines. A band of single pink roses and pink roses with another flower connected by a wavy green foliate line with small blue florets and various buds. A few blue floret sprigs. Pl. 232.

3324 Gold edge and border lines. Fawn background overdecorated with a large mazarine and light blue leaf and mazarine blue leaves all outlined in gold, also large pink roses, other flowers, and leaves. Pl. 233.

3371 Yellow edge and border line. Moulded floral sprays. Central large

polychrome floral spray in which a pink rose predominates.

3502 (Unconfirmed attribution.) An iron-red arched border band overdecorated with blue and magenta flowers and green leaves. There are similarly coloured sprays beneath the arches and scattered over the main body.

3639 3306, 3669 seem identical. Gold edge and border line. A simple floral band comprised of pink roses, yellow pansies, small blue daisies, other flowers and buds, green leaves.

3669 3306, 3639 seem identical. Gold edge and border line. A simple floral band comprised of pink roses, yellow pansies, small blue daisies, other flowers and buds, green leaves. Pl. 234.

3829 A foliate overgilt broad cream band with gilt scrolled lower edge and gilt scrolled quadrifoil cartouches containing flowers. Above is a narrow band of small polychrome rural scenes. Pl. 235.

3903 Gold edge lines. A simple undulating line of leaves and flowers in shades of mauve. Scattered small sprays in similar colours. Pl. 236.

Patterns without Numbers

THE FOLLOWING DESCRIPTIONS, each of which has been allocated a reference prefixed U for unnumbered, are of patterns which either have no pattern numbers or for which the pattern numbers have not yet been discovered. Some of these descriptions refer to patterns which seem to be obvious replacements for other manufacturers (e.g. numbers 53 and 212).

An R adjacent to the reference number of an item denotes that a New Hall concentric ring mark has been seen on an item decorated with this pattern. Any subsequent number or numbers on the top line of an item are the pattern numbers or U-reference numbers of known similar or associated patterns mentioned in this or the preceding chapter. Occasionally this space has been used to cross-reference a class of wares rather than a similarity of patterns (e.g. presentation jugs).

All the descriptions in this section are printed in U-reference order which in no way gives an indication of date of manufacture.

U1 Gold edge. Narrow inner mazarine blue border with gold line either side, the inner one having been made up of one-directional hatching.

U2 Gold edge. Inner gold line with a mazarine blue line of one-directional hatching below it.

U3 Brown Duvivier painted rural scene. Pl. 237.

U4 Looped gold edge. Polychrome Duvivier painted rural scene.

U5 Gold edge. Brown line outer border. Swags in brown and gold with pendants at joins and spoked wheel devices between. Pl. 238.

U6 Gold edge. Inner gold border consisting of single crosses each made up of four leaves and central dot. These are separated by pairs of dots and trefoils. See p. 82.

U7 Gold edge. Two gold lines on either side of ovals, each of which contains a double barbed arrowhead device facing right. Pl. 239 and p. 82.

U8 Gold edge. Inner gold line with, below, laurel leaf ovals with central star connected by small wavy line of laurel with offshoots terminating in a star.

U9 Gold edge and inner gold border line, between which is a wavy line of stalk and leaves with offshoots all in gold.

U10 3 Pink band edged in darker pink with a central row of small darker pink circles with blue dots in middle. Main floral spray consists of a large pink rose with several smaller polychrome flowers etc.

U11 Gold edge. Aquamarine band between gold lines with a line of gold-edged white discs separated by small circles and dots each containing a horizontal gold wheat ear. A further gold arrowhead border.

U12 U38 Gold edge. Inner border of two gold lines separated by a line of blue circles with gold centres. Main motif is a gold floral spray with two flowers and leaves, other gold sprigs. Pl. 240.

U13 Gold edge. Inner border of two gold lines separated by gold ovals within which are side-on five-point mavbe fleur-de-lis. Occasional small mavbe cartouches containing poly-chrome rose sprigs.

U15 Magenta edge. Dark blue inner border. Magenta line from which hang green leaf swags with single orange flowerlet at lowest point.

U16 Several almost identical patts. Blue edge line from which hang floral swags consisting of two magenta roses with a yellow flower one side and an orange one the other with a little green foliage.

U17 Several almost identical patts. Blue edge line from which hang floral swags consisting of a magenta rose, green foliage, and a single small mavbe daisy either side.

U18 Several almost identical patts. Blue edge line from which hang floral swags consisting of three magenta roses, green foliage, and a small yellow flower either side.

U19 Several almost identical patts. Blue edge line from which hang floral swags consisting of a magenta rose, a pink rose, green foliage with an orange flower one side and a yellow one the other.

U20 Pink border band with darker edge lines and overpainted ovals in a zigzag motif, below are small loops with trefoils. Main floral spray of magenta rose, mavbe flower, blue harebells, and green foliage. Pl. 241.

U21 Gold edge. Two gold border lines between which is a band of gold ovals with blobs at junctions and at the bottom also gold dots. A further small arched gold line with single dots under. See p. 82.

U23 U24 (Also in green.) Gold edge and border lines. Blue swags and pendants overgilt and suspended from gold discs. Pl. 242.

U24 U23 (Also in blue.) Gold edge and border lines. Green swags and pendants overgilt and suspended from gold discs. Pl. 243.

U25 84 Gold edge and border lines. Brown line with brown three leaf sprigs alternately either side. An undulating gold line with single flowerlet offshoots is superimposed.

U27 Gold edge and lower toothed line between which is a pale blue border which is overpainted with a tight band of pink roses, other small polychrome flowers, and green foliage. Very high quality. Col. Pl. M.

U28 Gold edge and border lines. Duvivier painted scene of a group of children in foreground with a house in the background. Colours not known.

U29 Green edge. Iron-red border band with central row of interconnected white diamonds and central line. Floral spray of large pink flower, three blue harebells, mauve flower, and green leaves etc. Pl. 244.

U30 Gold edge and border lines. A gold border set between a pair of gold lines consists of two sets of crossing looped lines, the loop junctions of one set end in tridents, the other in blobs. Col. Pl. J. See p. 82.

U31 264, 280, 288 Gold edge and border line. An undulating line of alternate black and gold tridents with gold and magenta pairs of dots (identical to patt. 288). With armorial.

U32 Gold edge and inner gold border line. Central black and white print of fruit. Several small prints of fruit.

U33 Gold edge and border lines. Pairs of gold leaf swags with pendants between joined by crossed blue and gold feather devices with rings over. Small vases of flowers in yellow and magenta above pendants.

U34 Gold edge and border line. Inner looped border in orange and black from which hang solid gold swags with gilt leaf pendants and black trefoils interspersed.

U35 Gold edge and border lines. A salmon pink gold-edged band has two undulating lines of gold foliage wound about it. Gold dots between swags. Gold sprigs.

U36 Gold edge and border lines with inner green line. Two pairs of gold border lines separated by gold cross-shaped devices made up of four dots and dashes. These are split into groups by brackets. Pl. 245.

U38 U12 Gold edge and border lines. A gold-edged mazarine blue band is overdecorated with connected gold circles with centre dots. An inner border of gold arrowheads and interspersed dots.

U39 208 Black border line. Inner border of mauve arrowheads crossed by an undulating line of iron-red dots. Central spray of two pink roses, one large green leaf, lesser polychrome foliage and flowers. Sprigs.

U40 U295 Gold edge and border line. Mazarine blue gold-edged band. An undulating line of gold foliage crosses this band from just above to well below it. Pl. 246.

U41 Gold edge and border line. A gold-edged mazarine blue band is overdecorated with pairs of diagonal gold lines alternating with a single diagonal line of gold dots. See p. 82.

U42 (Worcester replacement?) Gold edge and border line. A gold edged green band with gold loops and inverted V and dot device below. A narrow plain green band which has an undulating line of gold foliage passing behind it.

U43 Gold edge and border lines. A narrow gold border flat on top but with simple arch of leaves and long plain pendants below. See p. 83.

U44 142, 148 Gold edge and border line below which is an undulating line of iron-red feathers crossed by an undulating line of gold dots with large dots at joins. Two gold lines. All over iron-red and gold sprigs.

U47 Gold edge and border lines. A narrow mid blue band which has a gold band of wheat ears and green leaves entwined about it. A further gold line beneath.

U48 Gold edge and border line. A gold border flat at top and arched below with single dot under centre and angled pendant leaf fronds at ends. See p. 83.

U50 Gold edge/border lines. Broad gold band with overlapping serrated edge white leaf cut-outs. Veins etc. are left in gold so as to give a feather effect. Gold line below with loops and pendants. Marked: Cotton High Street Edinburgh. Chamberlains Worcester version is patt. no. 344. Col. Pl. H.

U51 Gold edge and border lines. All-over decoration of gold stars alternating with gold dots. See p. 83.

U52 (Not confirmed.) Two iron-red border lines with zigzag line beneath. Polychrome swags of small flowers and leaves. Main spray of two pink roses, small flowerlets, and green foliage.

U53 Gold edges and borders. Uneven green border edged with gold scrolls. Main motif is polychrome fruit and leaves with insects. Copy of Dr Wall Worcester.

U54 U108 Gold edges and border lines. Gold border of alternate pairs of leaves and berries. Broad band of wheel devices with central star separated by seaweed and leaves. Description uncertain.

U55 Mauve border band and lower line with looped line and trefoils below. Main spray of mauve and orange flowers, blue harebells, and green foliage.

U56 Green edge. Looped orange border band with dots between and line under. Main spray of pink and mauve flowers, blue harebells, and green foliage.

U57 171 Iron-red border of two parallel lines separated by an arched line with flowerlets at the junctions and hatched device between. Inner wavy line border. Centre low iron-red basket of polychrome blooms.

U58 Iron-red border of two parallel lines separated by an arched line with flowerlets at the junctions and hatched device between. Central spray of pink rose and other flowers. Lesser polychrome sprays.

U59 Border of two black lines separated by iron-red arrowheads. Inner border of a touching black and brown line which is crossed by an undulating magenta tendril with flowerlets. Interspersed green leaf.

U60 Iron-red border line with small loops and tridents beneath. Main floral spray of pink rose, yellow-centred iron-red flower, yellow bud and green foliage, etc. Lesser sprays.

U61 78, 273 Pink scale border between thick and thin magenta lines broken by scroll devices of magenta leaves with centre pendant of three green leaves. Simple spray of two differing iron-red flowers, green leaves. Pl. 247.

U62 Pale green edge. Magenta band with darker borders and over-decoration of an angled wavy line with two cross dashes. Beneath are filled-in magenta arches with pendant dotted lines. Pl.248.

U63 Border is a magenta line broken by plain scrolls. Main spray of large centre rose surrounded by five smaller roses all in magenta with mauve foliage. Pl. 249.

U64 Border of two blue lines separated by a row of blue circles with breaks for iron-red scroll work. Main scene is of the blue 'magic fungus' with iron-red fence, pink flowers, and polychrome foliage. Pl. 250.

U65 Overall dark blue background broken by silver lustre outlined cartouches and border lines. The cartouches contain black and white classical prints.

U66 Gold edge and border line. Plain dark blue band. Gold floral spray.

U67 Gold edge and border lines. Beneath a gold line a border of zigzag mazarine blue gilt-edged ovals with gold tridents between and pendants below. A further line with arched line and dots below, all gold. Pl. 251.

U68 Gold edge and border lines. A border of gold-edged mazarine blue scrolls with gilt fan-like devices and pendants between. Pl. 252.

U69 U289 Gold edge and border line. Gold-edged mazarine blue band overdecorated with an undulating line of scrolled gold leaves. See p. 83.

U70 Gold edge and border line. A gold-edged mazarine blue band with a tightly-spaced line of tiny leaves wound loosely about it and overdecorated with offshoot scrolls of larger leaves. Pl. 253.

U71 Gold dentate edge. Gold-edged mazarine blue band overdecorated with central gold line and pairs of leaves and white dots. Gold trefoils beneath. A narrow mazarine blue gold-edged band with gold sprigs over.

U73 White-dotted pale blue border with brown edges overdecorated with diamond-like devices in two shades of brown with dark blue dot centres. Inner border: wavy line of blue dots and small gold swags.

U74 Gold edge and border lines. Gold-edged brown border with concave curves on top edge. Gold sprigs etc. above. Inner wavy border of connected gold ticks.

U76 Gold edge. Mazarine blue gold-edged band overdecorated with pairs of diagonal gold lines interspersed with ovals. Gold line with undulating tendril of gold foliage around it.

U77 Gold edge and border line. Gold-edged mazarine blue band overdecorated in gold by ovals and with two undulating lines of foliage entwined around it.

U78 U276 Gold edge and border lines. Mazarine blue border with arches on lower side and overgilt with four-dot device which is repeated on the body. Small pendants. A further gold-edged mazarine blue band. Pl. 254.

U79 Black edge. Slightly shaped mazarine blue border with black fan-like pendants alternating with simple pendants under. A further border of black arrowheads. Spray of black wheat ears. Pl. 255.

U80 Gold edge and border lines. Mazarine blue border overgilt with small wavy line of foliage with small gold blobs and pendants under gold border line. Small gold sprays of foliage.

U81 170, U112, U272 Gold edge and border line. Mazarine blue scrolls connected by circles with gold centres and outlined in gold, crossed by an undulating line of small gold crossed line devices and dots. Col. Pl. L.

U82 Gold edge and border lines. A line of gold arrow-heads. Gold-edged mazarine blue band with another gold line either side overdecorated with crossing gold ovals and dots, broken by cross device in brackets. Pl. 256.

U83 Gold edge and border lines. A narrow pink band with gold edges the lower being arched with pendant crossing leaves and horizontal leaves. A polychrome rural print within a gold cartouche. Pl. 257.

U84 Gold edge and border line. A polychrome Adam Buck print. Pl. 258.

U86 Gold edge. Two pairs of gold parallel lines between which are two pairs of gold zigzag parallel lines with blue dashes. Gold sprigs.

U87 302, 329, 357, U98 Gold edge and border line. Band of brown oak leaves and acorns in pairs and singles, all facing outwards, overgilt. Pl. 259.

U88 Gold edge and border line. Black line with black Greek key pattern under and a wavy line of black dots overgilt with swags. Large overgilt floral spray.

U89 Gold base border line. Sparse black spray of one rose and two hips with leaves.

U91 Yellow edge, green band with magenta lower edge and line and bottom border line. Another line in blue. Polychrome floral spray and gold monogram.

U93 272, 274, 360, 490, 856, U183, U301 Gold edge and border lines. 'Tobacco' pattern in plain blue and orange, some green, with gilt edges. The complex top border in blue and orange is NOT gilded.

U94 Gold edge and border line. Broad mazarine blue band

overdecorated with large bloom in scale pink and pale pink. Large white leaf. Green leaf. Three smallish orange flowers. All overgilt. Pl. 260.

U95 Gold edge. All-over orange background. Several large white flowers with yellow centres surrounded either by dots or small tridents. Two-tone individual green leaves. Some overgilding.

U96 Gold edge and border line. Broad mazarine blue band overdecorated with heavy white scrolls and large white and orange buds all overgilt and with gold foliage. Pl. 261.

U97 Gold edge and border lines. Overall orange colour with gold scalloped lower edge. Large formalized almost square white flower with small white flower in centre gold ring. The whole is overgilt. Pl. 262.

U98 302, 329, 357, U87 Gold edge and border lines. A band of individual two-tone green or blue oak leaves with groups of two or three fawn and brown acorns. Gold tendrils and leaf outlines.

U99 Gold edge and border lines. Main motif of a mazarine blue leaf in centre of scroll of small orange leaves, repeated. Under are two different crossing gold leaf swags. Above other gold and mazarine blue motifs. Pl. 263.

U100 Mainly silver lustre. A narrow wavy band of leaves crossed by a dotted wavy line. A broad band of three parallel lines, the centre being crossed by an undulating line of trefoils and red berries on sprigs.

U101 Mainly silver lustre. Broad scrolled band of foliage between orange and silver lines with large orange bud, orange scroll centres, and connecting fronds. A few greeny/brown leaves at top.

U102 Mainly silver lustre. Border bands. Wide central band with orange line at top, arched line with swags, and orange flower below and central four-leaf figure. A further foliate band below. Pl. 264.

U103 Silver lustre edge and band. A band of silver leaves and orange flowers above an orange line. Central bouquet of orange flowers and silver lustre leaves.

U104 Silver edge. Inner mazarine blue line and Japan-style shrub with orange flowers and buds and silver lustre foliage and outline.

U105 Silver edge and border line. Broad band of three diagonal orange flowers with silver foliage separated by sprays of silver lustre leaves with one orange leaf. Pl. 265.

U106 Silver edge and border lines. A broad zigzag band between silver and orange lines consists of broad orange band with dots connected to the next by a pair of thin orange lines and silver squiggle. Silver sprays. Pl. 266.

U107 1313, U209 Silver edge and border line. Japan-style overall decoration consists of a mazarine blue bush with orange berries and a single small orange flower outlined in and overdecorated with silver fronds. Pl. 267.

U108 U54 Silver edge. A broad band between silver lines consists of a round device with central formalized bloom with orange centre and silver radial lines separated by orange leaf device and silver tendrils.

U109 Gold edge. Large sprays of two or three flowers in magenta and yellow or magenta and blue, with green foliage.

U110 Gold edge and border line. Overall mid blue marbled effect crazed with fine gold lines. Same decoration in and outside. Pl. 268.

U112 170, U81, U272 Border band of plain mazarine blue joined scrolls with an undulating line of magenta arrowheads superimposed. A few polychrome sprigs.

U113 443, 521 Gold edge. A group of six feather-like leaves and similar three-, four- and five-pointed leaves in dotted orange with sprays of mauve berries. Overgilding with angled straight lines and tendrils. Pl. 269.

U114 Blue edge and border lines. Broad blue border with green star devices and ripple effect. Iron-red vertical bands with blue loops one side and pendants both. Polychrome floral spray, magenta roses.

U115 435, 436, U118–20, U250, U284–6 Gold edged border of rectangular cartouches with pink

vertical dividers alternately containing hand-painted rural scenes and gold diamonds. Zigzag gold border under. Fine floral spray.

U116 U115, U118–20, U250, U284–6 Gold edge and border lines. Rural scene containing grey and brown cows.

U117 Gold edge and border lines. A double border band (colour unknown) with arched lower edge and pendant leaves. A circular cartouche containing a scene of a church-like and other buildings (colour unknown).

U118 U115–16, U119–20, U250, U284–6 Gold edge and border lines. Large well-painted floral spray containing very detailed flowers in pink, orange, yellow, and orange and finely-shaded leaves in various tones of green etc.

U119 U115–16, U118, U120, U250, U284–6 Gold edge and border lines. Broad gold border in Greek key pattern. Very large and detailed floral spray. (Colours unknown.)

U120 U115–16, U118–19, U250, U284–6 Gold edge and border lines. Broad vine leaf and bunches of grapes border. Duvivier painted scenes containing birds. Colours are browns and greens.

U121 Gold edge and border line. Overgilt mazarine blue half leaves, in two sizes, suspended from edge. Swags of gold and orange foliage suspended between alternate leaves. Pl. 270.

U122 Gold edge. Overall decoration consists of stalk of mazarine blue leaves and bloom with various other flowers of different sizes in orange with tendrils and small green leaves.

U123 1126, 1218, 1304, 1318, 1378, 1413 Gold edge and borders. Two mazarine blue bands, overgilt with diagonal lines and dots, either side of broad light blue band overdecorated with large pink and orange flowers, green/white gilt leaves.

U125 U282 Magenta edge and border line. A floral band comprised of two pink flowers, one orange flower, pairs of blue flowers all with yellow centres, plus lesser flowers and green leaves. Poor quality painting.

U126 Gold edge and border line. Large mazarine blue three-pointed leaf with large white and orange flower attached. Other mauve, magenta, and orange flowers and small green leaves complete overall decoration.

U128 (Attribution doubtful.) Gold edge and border lines. Inner arched mazarine blue border with gold pendants and blue rectangular devices at points. Pairs of pink roses with green leaves and gold tendrils.

U129 Black edge and border line. Broad pale blue band overdecorated with a black rural print.

U130 U131, U194, U213, U270, U281 Gold edge and border lines etc. Moulded hunting scene in white on a pale blue background. Moulded wavy line foliage border band.

U131 U130, U194, U213, U270, U281 Moulded hunting scene with polychrome overdecoration. Border band is a straight black stalk with pairs of green leaves and pairs of stalks with three orange berries.

U132 Gold edge and border lines. Wavy band of gold foliage. Broad mazarine blue band decorated with large white and gold oak leaves interspersed with gold foliage.

U133 All over gold only decoration. Zigzag border of leaves. A dotted gold band with solid middle lines wavy-edged at the bottom and scrolled at the top. Above alternately are grenade and tulip devices. Pl. 271.

U135 R White flower moulded border on pale blue background. Gold edges and border lines. Polychrome rural print.

U136 Basket-weave border. Cartouches contain different sprays of flowers. Main spray contains yellow, magenta, iron-red, and blue flowers with green foliage. Naively painted.

U137 Gold edges and border lines. Polychrome rural print.

U138 Gold edges and border lines. Moulded white flower border on all-over blue background. Overgilt broad border of single large pink flowers with green leaves. Narrow mazarine blue band overgilt.

U139 Gold edges and border lines. Broad salmon pink band over-decorated with iron-red flowers, dark green single leaves, and gold foliage.

U140 1478, U271 Gold edge and border lines. White moulded flower border on blue background. Centre spray contains pink, blue, and yellow flowers with green leaves. Polychrome sprigs. Pl. 272.

U141 Gold edge and inner border of wavy line foliage. White bird moulded border on green background. Central polychrome spray of fruit.

U142 Blue edge with black line. Pink border band overdecorated with darker pink leaves and dots. Main spray: large yellow and pink daisy-like flowers and green leaves. Polychrome sprigs.

U143 Gold edge and border lines. Bird moulded border is all white. Large bouquet with big flowers mainly in dark reds and pink, with some orange and blue. Green leaves. Good quality decoration.

U144 Gold edge and border lines. Bird moulded border all in white. Main spray of flowers is in yellow, pink, and mauve with green foliage. Lesser sprays have blue and pink flowers.

U145 (Doubtful attribution.) Gold edge and border line. White flower moulded border on pale blue background. Central single large blue flower with yellow centre and green leaves.

U146 Brown edge and border line. Polychrome decorated flower moulded border on a plain white background.

U147 Gold edge and border lines. A foliate border band in light blue and gold. A formalized overall scroll and leaf motif in mazarine blue, light blue, orange, and iron-red with much overgilding.

U148 3 Arched magenta edge line with a parallel mauve looped line beneath and pendant trefoils. A spray of four pink blooms in graduated sizes, one mauve bloom, a stem of blue harebells, and some green foliage. Col. Pl. N.

U149 1126, 1218, 1304, 1318, 1378, 1413 Gold edge and border lines. Two mazarine blue bands overgilt with angled 'f's. Broad light blue border between with alternate pink pompoms and pink and white blooms, green leaves, and small gold sprays. Pl. 273.

U150 Mazarine blue border band with overgilt edge and zigzag leaf stems. Overall mid blue background with single magenta fading to white flowers, sprays of three green leaves, many tiny orange flowers. Pl. 274.

U151 1126, 1218, 1304, 1318, 1378, 1413 Gold edge and border lines. Two mazarine blue borders overgilt with single leaves between which is a light blue band with alternate face-on white flowers and angled pale pink flowers with green leaves. Pl. 275.

U152 570, 572, 752 Gold edges. Border of pairs of two gold leaves in arrow formation. Chinese-style scene, central beehive, building and tree to right, floral bush to left. Mainly in mazarine blue and orange heavily overgilt. Pl. 276.

U154 R Gold edge. Green border band with darker overdecoration. Main motif consists of large single two-tone orange flowers with a bud and dark green leaves. Some green sprigs.

U155 Gold edge and border line. A border of pink roses separated by three green leaves, a gold fern leaf, and gold foliage. Pl. 277.

U156 Gold edge. Main large bouquet of pink roses and rosebuds, other various flowers in pink, orange, mauve, and blue with green foliage. Similar smaller sprays with alternate gold sprays used as a border.

U157 Gold edge and border lines, other colours unknown. A broad band of large square cartouches alternately containing scenes of figures and floral bouquets.

U158 Gold edge and border line. Broad border of single mauve daisies interspersed with single pink and white flowers, both with yellow centres, separated by green leaves and stems of blue flowers.

U159 Gold edge and border line. A border of pink flowers, in various tones, with yellow centres, one pair and the rest as singles at different angles. Green leaves and gold tendrils separate them. Pl. 278.

U160 Gold edge and border lines. White flower moulded border. Central decoration is a large magenta shell, two smaller orange shells, and a few green fronds.

U161 Gold edge and border lines. White flower moulded border. Central decoration is a botanical painting of different types of green leaves.

U162 Gold edge. White bird moulded border on all over pale blue background. Inner and centre overgilt mazarine blue band. Main motif: alternate magenta and orange daisies separated by green leaves and a bud.

U163 (Attribution doubtful.) Dark brown edge and border line. Brown rural scene prints.

U164 984 Gold edge and border line. Fine quality polychrome rural prints in soft colours. Pl. 279.

U165 Gold edge and border line. Magenta armorial of a stag and monogram JM.

U167 R Gold edge and border lines. Main motif is Chinese-style exotic animals in bright blue, orange, and yellow with other complex decoration and much overgilding. (Chamberlains Worcester patt. 75.) Pl. 280.

U168 R 1541 Gold edge and dark blue border, Chinese-style scene, all in dark and light blue, showing a building in the centre, tree to the right, flowering shrub left, and a bridge and rocks in the foreground. Pl. 281.

U169 R Gold edge. Mauve rural print. Pl. 282.

U170 R Gold edge and wavy stem leaf border. Oriental scene, in mazarine and light blue with orange and much overgilding, showing building to the right, bridge centre, tree left, and two people in foreground. Pl. 283.

U171 Moulded border of leaves and berries in black, orange, and green. Moulded scene of cherubs leading a beast. Colours are green, blue, brown, and skin pink. Pl. 284.

U172 R 2488 Gold edge and border line. Light blue reversed Willow Pattern type scene with two persons on the bridge and no doves.

U173 R Gold edge. White oak-leaf moulded border. Overall pale blue background with white moulded cherubs leading a beast.

U174 R Gold edge. White flower moulded border on pale blue band. Central motif is a polychrome rural print. Pl. 285.

U175 Blue and white Willow Pattern style print with one person on the bridge and two in the foreground. With and without gold edge and border line. Pl. 286.

U176 Gold edge and border lines. Blue and white Willow Pattern style print with one person on the bridge and one in the foreground. Pl. 287.

U177 570 Scene of a house and a tree crudely painted in shades of dark blue. (Possibly unfinished patt. 570.) Pl. 288.

U178 U294 Blue and white scene of flowering shrubs and two flying doves. Gold edge and border line with band of gold circles and centre dots between gold lines.

U179 Blue and white so called 'Ducks' pattern which shows a pagoda and fence with a number of ducks and fishing boats. May be overgilded. Pl. 289.

U180 Very dark blue/black painted scene of a house, a long criss-cross fence, trees and shrubs with a fungus type growth in foreground. Cross-hatched border (see next). Pl. 290.

U181 Bright blue painted scene of a house, a long zigzag cross-design fence, trees and shrubs with fungus type growth in foreground (see previous).

U182 Hand-painted mid blue and white decoration. Border of complex design has a zigzag lower edge. Main decoration consists of differing small sprays of flowers. Pl. 291.

U183 272, 274, 360, 490, 856, U93, U301 'Tobacco' pattern in various shades of mid and dark blue.

U184 Blue and white 'Moths' pattern includes pagodas, trees, and boat.

U185 473 Blue and white 'Twisted Tree' pattern also contains a large pagoda to the right, a small one in the background, and a small boat left foreground. Col. Pl. M, Pl. 292.

U186 Blue and white oriental-style scene of two children playing near a large urn. An even larger urn is also a main part of the design. Col. Pl. E.

U187 Blue and white oriental-type scene of a 'Gazebo' in a cleft rock. A boat also appears below in the foreground. (Also appears gilded.)

U188 Gold edge and border line. Pale blue and white oriental scene of two people under a pagoda on pillars. Another pagoda with two people outside and another in a window. A lot of shrubbery. Pl. 293.

U189 Blue and white oriental-type scene of a pagoda to the left, a multitiered pagoda right rear, and a boat in the foreground.

U190 Blue edge line. Light magenta band with darker overdecoration of arrows and dots. Below are small dark magenta scroll and pendants. A simple polychrome spray of flowers completes the decoration. Pl. 294.

U191 Gold edge and border lines. Blue and white oriental type scene known as the 'Trench Mortar' or 'Guns' pattern is comprised of a large building fronted by a number of tubes, a bridge, rocks and trees, etc. Pl. 295.

U193 Gold edge. A few apple-green differing leaf sprays.

U194 U130, U131, U213, U270, U281 White moulded hunting scene on overall green background. Border band is a straight stalk with pairs of leaves and pairs of stalks with three berries all in white on green ground.

U195 Gold edge and border lines with tiny loops and larger hatched loops facing inwards. Between are single orange and black hips with gold foliage and ovals with mauve dot. Beneath is a band of angled gold leaves. Pl. 296.

U196 Gold edge and border line. Decoration comprised of a well-painted single large pink rose on a stem of four green leaves hanging down. A few small sprigs.

U197 Gold edge and border lines. A narrow band of gold interlocking ovals, each with three dots, broken by small cartouches containing spray of blue flowers and green leaves.

U199 Mid blue dentil-edge band. Straight magenta stem, alternate pairs of yellow and green leaves.

U200 Gold edge and border line. Broad band of four-petal yellow flowers with brown tufts alternating with magenta-edged flowers with dotted centres. Two-tone green leaves.

U201 Gold dentil-edge band. Polychrome paintings of children or still life.

U202 Brown edge. Iron-red wavy border line forms occasional bows. Main spray: large blue daisy at centre, stem of magenta flowers, stem of red and yellow daisies. Second spray has rose and iron-red daisies. Pl. 297.

U203 Basket-weave moulding. Blue background. Cartouches contain two orange daisies with gold centres and leaves. White centre or base is edged by orange pansies with gold centres and leaves. Gold edge lines.

U206 Orange edge. Border of alternate blue and green angled ovals connected by iron-red sprigs. Some large iron-red flowers and green leaves sprout from a large blue device in front of an iron-red fence.

U207 Brown edge and inner border line. A wavy line of two-tone single green leaves which are joined by a small wavy line of iron-red sprigs.

U208 Gold edge. An undulating gold stem connects single feathery five-pointed leaves with gold tendrils and pairs of bunches of orange berries.

U209, 1313, U107 Gold edge. Large Japan-style plant in mazarine blue. Overall stems of harebell-type orange flowers with narrow green leaves.

U210 Gold edge. A broad border, mainly in gold, of pairs of fern-like leaves in > formation separated by single orange and black flowerlets with a single orange and black bud, all with gold stems. Pl. 298.

U211 Gold edge and border lines. Broad band of gold cross-hatched feather-like trident devices. The gold foliate pendant suspended from each connecting point has three orange flowerlets. Pl. 299.

U212 (Chamberlains replacement?) Gold edge and border lines. Mazarine blue border bands. Very broad band of joined seaweed fronds in mazarine

blue edged with gold and with gold tendrils. (Chamberlains Worcester pattern.)

U213 U130, U131, U194, U270, U281 Brown edge. Moulded hunting scene with polychrome overdecoration. Border band is a straight brown stalk with pairs of green leaves and pairs of stalks with three orange berries.

U214 Gold edge and border lines. A band of mazarine blue dentil-edged circular devices outlined and overdecorated in gold. Connecting decoration of bottom swags, dots, top loops, and foliage all in gold.

U215 U245 Gold edge. Border band of small gold disks between a pair of gold lines. Undulating gold line of alternate single leaves and berries over a straight gold line. See p. 83.

U216 Iron-red border bands. An undulating line of blue arrowheads crossed by an undulating dotted-edged and cross-hatched ribbon. There is a single rose and leaves in each cartouche so formed.

U217 Gold edge and border lines with brown band between overlaid with a wavy green line, white ovals, green and magenta swags below. A few small sprigs of various fruits.

U218 U226, U260, U262 Gold edge. Overall pale blue ground. White moulded vine edge band. Large single white moulded leaves interspersed with white moulded hollyhock stems.

U219 (Worcester replacement?) Gold edge and border lines. Narrow looped orange border band. 'Quail' pattern depicting a pair of quails with one orange and two blue flowers, a stump, and sparse foliage.

U221 Gold edges, name, date, and spout decoration. Light blue moulded vine edge band. Light blue moulded decoration of chariot scenes, etc.

U222 Gold edge and border lines. Wavy gold foliate border band. Orange panels with gold flower in centre of diamond device. Black panels with circular device of gold petals with orange centre.

U223 Gold edges and border lines. Wavy gold foliate border. Heavily overgilded mazarine blue background with single large pink and yellow flowers. Inner panels with orange flowers, mazarine blue and green leaves.

U224 (Doubtful attribution.) Scent bottle with hand-painted polychrome prints of known New Hall black and white prints.

U225 Gold edge and line. Polychrome decorated moulding. Pink roses, blue flowers, magenta edged flowers with yellow centres and green leaves. Pl. 300.

U226 U218, U252, U260, U262 Overall pale lavender blue ground. White vine moulded edge band. Large white moulded acanthus leaves interspersed with white moulded harebell stems.

U227 Named presentation jug. Double border band in fawn and

mazarine blue with gold edges. Large mixed bunch of flowers in various colours (this appears to have been added at a later date).

U229 Gold edge and border lines. Broad orange band overgilded with diamond devices and scrollwork etc.

U231 Gold edge and border lines. Broad mazarine blue band overdecorated with thick gold foliate scrollwork.

U232 Gold edge and border lines. Broad orange band overdecorated with gold Greek key pattern.

U233 U235 Gold edge and border lines. Mazarine blue border band overdecorated with a line of connected gold discs. A gold tendril of single leaves and berries entwined about a single straight gold line.

U234 Gold edge and border lines. A border of gold arrowheads and dots between gold lines. All in brown, a narrow border of a pair of lines separated by dots over a wavy line of dots. Brown and gold sprays. Pl. 301.

U235 U233 Gold edge and border lines. Mazarine blue border band overdecorated with a line of connected gold circles and dots. A gold tendril of single leaves and berries entwined about a single straight gold line.

U236 Gold edge and border lines. Mazarine blue border band overdecorated with a line of joined gold leaf sprays. Swags of gold pendants and dots separated by scrolls and broad pendants. Gold leaf sprays above. Pl. 302.

U237 Gold edge and border lines. Band or bands of single pink roses alternating with buds and separated by five green leaves. (Similar to Charles Bourne pattern.)

U238 Gold edge and border lines. Border band of connected gold discs. Mazarine blue border overgilded with a right-angled zigzag line and a pattern of scrolls and harebells.

U239 Gold edge and border lines. A border of three-pointed leaves separated by a berry either side of a straight line. All in gold. See p. 83.

U241 Wavy line border of mauve dots. Mauve floral spray of which the main flower has an orange centre. Mauve sprigs.

U242 Gold edges and border bands. Narrow border and inner mazarine blue bands decorated with gold leaves. Pale green ground with octagonal polychrome floral cartouches. Mazarine blue and orange spray. Gold tendrils.

U243 1109, 1147, 1178, 1236, 1277, 1525 Edge, border line, and 1815 dated monogram all in gold. Puce-coloured Adam Buck mother and child print. Pl. 303.

U244 Basket weave. Broad outer and narrow inner gold bands. The cartouches contain differing sprays of flowers including a single pink rose, forget-me-nots, and other flowers in orange and mauve, green leaves.

U245 U215 Gold edge. Border band of small gold circles with central dots between a pair of gold lines. Undulating gold line of alternate single leaves and berries over a straight gold line. See p. 83.

U246 1874 Blue border bird moulded. Two inner bands of gilt mazarine blue, between is a line of large well-painted pink roses with green leaves on white background. A similar rose decorates centre.

U247 Gold edge. Green foliate swags. Gold sprigs. Various polychrome insects.

U248 Gold edge and border lines. Gold leaf and berry border band. Overall decoration comprised of a scattering of a large single pink rose with bud and green leaves. Scattered gold leaf sprigs.

U249 Gold edge and border lines. Border of alternate moulded and polychrome floral sprays. Main spray consists of a pink rose and bud, a sprig of blue harebells and mixed flowers with green foliage.

U250 U115–16, U118–20, U284–6 Blue edge and border lines. Border of blue arrowhead swags and pendants. Moulded leaves outlined in green hatching with brown stems. Large polychrome floral spray in centre of each leaf.

U251 U292 Gold edge and border lines. Border band of concentric mazarine blue and gold semicircles with lighter blue dots. All are outlined in gold with the lower edges feathered. Lower half loop-moulded. Pl. 304.

U252 U218, U226 White vine moulded edge band. Large green moulded acanthus leaves interspersed with blue and brown moulded harebell stems. Broad green lower border band.

U253 Gold edge and border line. Border of line of magenta dots above pair of iron-red lines. Below is wavy dotted magenta line with alternate magenta and gold sprigs and gold sprigs. Main spray magenta and gold. Pl. 305.

U254 Mazarine blue panels with two iron-red daisies alternate with white panels with mazarine blue cross. Floral decoration in iron-red and green. Circles on a broad mazarine blue squiggle. All overgilded. Pl. 306.

U256 Gold edge and border lines. Wavy border of gold leaves and dots. A border of single large blue harebells with gold stems and four small magenta appendages. Each is separated by a large thin gold leaf. Pl. 307.

U257 Orange edge. The sparse decoration consists of a crude single iron-red flower and bud with three or four green leaves.

U258 (From poor photograph.) Gold edges and overgilding. Oriental-style scene. Large tree to left, slender tree to right, central building with fence to right, and V-shaped fence in foreground. Colours: mazarine blue, green, and orange.

U259 686 Pink scale border with darker edge lines and a line of small mauve arches with trefoils at joints. The main spray has a large mauve rose, a large pink flower, iron-red and yellow flowers, green leaves.

U260 U218, U226, U262 A blue moulded floral spray with a protruding flower either side, on a white background. (N.H. pad-mark.) Pl. 308.

U261 Gold edge band and scroll-work border with hatched cartouche containing a gold clover leaf and a dotted cartouche containing a single pink rose.

U262 U218, U226, U260 White background with pale blue moulded decoration comprising a wavy floral border with hollyhock and other floral stems on the main body. (N.H. pad-mark.)

U263 Gold edges and edge lines. Pale green ground overdecorated with single large pink flowers which are separated by three small orange-edged white daisies and three buds. Black spriggy foliage.

U265 Bird moulded blue border. Inner mazarine blue band. Floral spray comprised of a yellow daisy, a pair of shaded iron-red flowers, a pair of pink roses, and scattered green leaves. Rather crude.

U266 1442, 1444 Blue edge. Main floral spray of a pink rose, mauve tulip, and other daisy-like flowers in blue, yellow, and red with green leaves. Sprays of various flowers.

U267 Gold edge and grape vine border band. Brightly-painted hunting scene of man with gun behind tree stump, two dogs, and a pheasant. Church etc. in background. Pl. 309.

U268 Gold edges. Maroon name, date, and spout decoration. White moulded vine edgeband on light blue ground. White moulded classical chariot scenes etc. on light blue ground. WOLVERHAMPTON 1836.

U269 Gold edge and central sprig. Border of a many-petalled faded blue flower with a dotted conical yellow centre alternating with a group of four leaves in faded green and yellow. Other foliage. Pl. 310.

U270 U130, U131, U194, U213, U281 Gold edge. Moulded hunting scene with polychrome overdecoration. Border band is a scrolled brown stalk with green leaves and alternate single blue and red blooms within the scrolls. Pl. 311.

U271 1478, U140 Gold edge. White moulded flower border on blue background. Central spray contains a puce and yellow tulip, a yellow flower with faded green leaves, and small flowers in various colours.

U272 170, U81, U112 Gold edge. Mazarine blue scrolls joined by gold circles with mazarine blue centres, crossed by an undulating line of gold discs. Single gold stars. Inner gold line with twisted tendril.

U273 Gold edge. A border band of slightly curved trellis work between parallel lines with single line under, all in gold apart from blue dots at intersections. A few gold leaf sprigs.

U274 R A light blue quail and an iron-red quail sitting together. The rest of the decoration consists of flowers and twigs also in light blue and iron-red. Simple and stylized. Pl. 312.

U275 1897, 1930 Basket weave moulding. Cartouches contain floral sprays in magenta, mid blue and iron-red with green and yellow leaves. Main spray has a large magenta rose, large blue flower, and a grey flower.

U276 U78 Gold edge and border lines. Mazarine blue border with arches on lower side overgilt with dots and stars. There are single gold stars within the arches with swags and dot pendants suspended beneath border.

U277 Gold edge and border line. Duvivier decorated sepia rural scene which includes three people with a dog, trees, and a ruin.

U278 1897, 1930, U275 Basket-weave. Cartouches contain either a pair of yellow-centred pink daisies, with or without three blue-edged yellow flowers, or a single daisy with three pink-edged yellow flowers.

U280 Gilt and puce decoration consists of two pairs of border lines separated by oval daisy medallions which are connected by swags. A further wavy foliate border band.

U281 U130, U131, U194, U213, U270 Gold edge. Overall raspberry pink background. White moulded hunting scene. Border band is a straight stalk with pairs of leaves and pairs of stalks with three berries all moulded in white.

U282 U125 A floral band comprised of two pink flowers, one orange flower, two different blue flowers all with yellow centres and connecting green foliage. Naive painting.

U283 R 1063 Mustard edge and border line. Puce rural prints. Pl. 313.

U284 U115, U116, U118–20, U250, U285–6 Gold edge and border lines. Puce transfer-printed 'THE FAR-MERS ARMS'.

U285 U115–16, U118–20, U250, U284, U286 Gold edge and border lines. Border of arrowhead swags and pendants. Duvivier painting of a rural scene.

U286 U115–16, U118–20, U250, U284, U285 Leaf moulding. Enamelled edge, a border line of blobs and pairs of dots. A plain line with plain swags and pendants under. A large floral spray and inscription 'Thomas Brundrell 1793'.

U287 Blue transfer-printed acanthus leaves. Pl. 314.

U288 Gold edge and border lines. Mazarine blue border overgilt with zigzag device. Scattered gold-edged mazarine blue stars and gold dots. Pl. 315.

U289 U69 Gold edge and lines. Crossing wavy gold foliage border.

Gold edged mazarine blue band overdecorated with an undulating line of scrolled gold leaves. A further mazarine blue border with gold trefoils. Pl. 316.

U290 Gold edge. Dark blue border band with polychrome floral swags suspended below. Pl. 317.

U291 Gold dentil edge and border line. Scattered magenta and green floral sprigs alternating with gold leaf sprigs. Pl. 318.

U292 U251 Border of dark blue concentric semicircles with magenta dots between and a magenta leaf and berry border line under. Pl. 319.

U293 Gold edge. Gold and polychrome floral border. Floral cartouche containing monogram. (Probable replacement.) Pl. 320.

U294 U178 Blue and white scene of flowering shrubs and two flying doves. Pl. 321.

U295 U40 Gold edge and border lines. Mazarine blue band overgilt with alternate arrowheads and dots. An undulating foliage line passes behind the band. There is a lower line of gold arrowheads and dots. Pl. 322.

U296 Cabbage-leaf moulding. Brown edge band with arcs and trefoils under. A wavy blue line with magenta swags and pendants suspended under it. Large polychrome floral spray. Pl. 323.

U297 Magenta edge line. Pairs of green garlands break the magenta border band which is overdecorated with a paler ribbon. Under each section of border is a single magenta quadrifoil with dots.

U298 A broad undulating floral band of individual pink roses separated by a blue four-petalled flower and green leaves and with elderberry spray above and below the flowers.

U299 934 Gold edge and border lines with mazarine blue band between. Black and white print of basket of flowers. Pl. 324.

U300 A pair of magenta border lines separated by alternate blue and magenta quadrifoil devices. A few blue and magenta sprigs on main body. Pl. 325.

U301 272, 274, 360, 490, 856, U93, U183 Silver lustred edge and border lines. 'Tobacco' pattern. Dark blue ground with green and iron-red leaves. The wheel-like device has a white background.

U302 1939 Gold edge and border line. Blue basket-weave moulded border band with floral cartouches and main floral spray in which the three larger flowers are magenta, yellow and khaki, and yellow. Pl. 326.

Sketches of Patterns

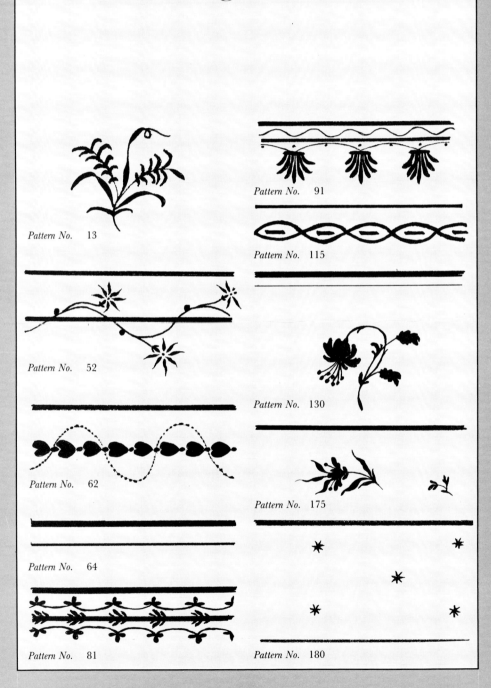

Pattern No.   13

Pattern No.   91

Pattern No.   115

Pattern No.   52

Pattern No.   130

Pattern No.   62

Pattern No.   175

Pattern No.   64

Pattern No.   81

Pattern No.   180

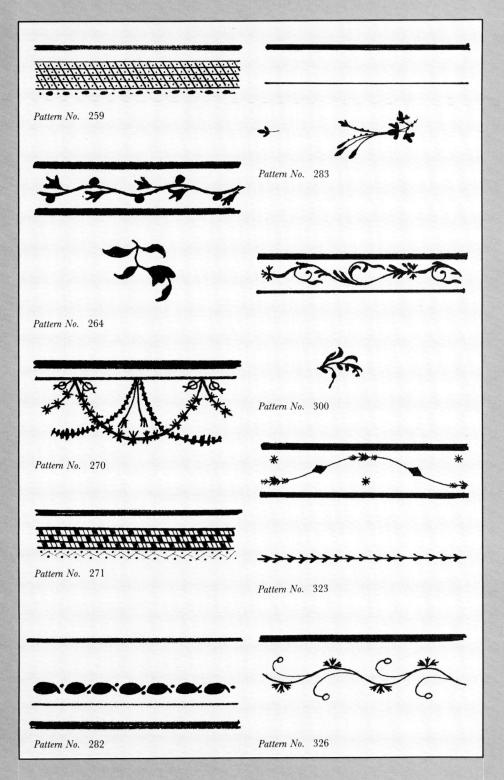

Pattern No. 259

Pattern No. 283

Pattern No. 264

Pattern No. 270

Pattern No. 300

Pattern No. 271

Pattern No. 323

Pattern No. 282

Pattern No. 326

Pattern No.   542

Reference No.   U6

Pattern No.   614

Reference No.   U7

Pattern No.   919

Reference No   U21

Pattern No. 1041

Reference No.   U30

Pattern No. 1055

Reference No.   U41

Reference No. U43

Reference No. U239

Reference No. U48

Reference No. U51

Reference No. U245

Reference No. U69

Reference No. U215

Bibliography

Charleston, R. J. and Towner, D., *English Ceramics 1580–1830* (Sotheby Parke Bernet, 1977)

Fisher, S. W., *Fine Porcelain and Pottery* (Octopus, 1974)

Godden, G. A., *An Illustrated Encyclopaedia of British Pottery and Porcelain* (Herbert Jenkins, 1966)

——, *British Porcelain* (Barrie & Jenkins, rev. edn 1986)

——, (ed.), *Staffordshire Porcelain* (Granada, 1983)

——, *Encyclopaedia of British Porcelain Manufacturers* (Barrie & Jenkins, 1988)

Holgate, D., *New Hall and Its Imitators* (Faber & Faber, 1971)

——, (ed. P. Halfpenny), *Bicentenary Exhibition Catalogue* (Stoke-on-Trent City Museum & Art Gallery, 1981)

——, *New Hall* (Faber & Faber, 1987)

Miller, P. and Berthoud, M., *An Anthology of British Teapots* (Micawber, 1985)

Rhead, G. W. and F. A., *Staffordshire Pots and Potters* (Hutchinson, 1906: EP, 1977)

Stringer, G. E., *New Hall Porcelain* (Art Trade Press, 1949)

Watney, B., *English Blue and White Porcelain of the 18th Century* (Faber & Faber, 1973)

Patterns Listed by Description Type Sequence

THIS SECTION LISTS THE New Hall pattern numbers, and my own U-series, according to a Description Type sequence which lists the major type headings, so as to assist in the allocation of pattern numbers to unmarked items. The sequence within the headings is as follows:

Blue and white
Monochrome Adam Buck and classical prints
Polychrome Adam Buck prints
Black and white rural prints
Monochrome rural prints
Polychrome rural prints
Hand-painted rural and other scenes
Black and white fruit
Polychrome fruit
Black and white floral
Black and white floral with coloured band
Dr Syntax
Simple polychrome borders
Duvivier decorated
Polychrome oriental scenes
Monochrome bands
Monochrome bands with over-decoration
Monochrome bands with over-decoration and floral sprays
Shells
Baskets
Tobacco patterns
Warburtons Patent

Armorial
Swags
Pink scale borders
Mainly gold with other colours
Simple monochrome patterns
Overall sprigs
Floral sprays
Primary background colour with overdecoration
Undulating or wavy line borders
Crossing undulating or wavy line borders
Late oriental-type scenes
Silver lustre
Bird scenes
Mazarine blue and gold
Marble effects
Strawberry and other fruit patterns
Bush and tree patterns
Geometric patterns
Circular devices
Exotic animals
Flowers in cartouches
Scenes in cartouches
Large leaf patterns
Large flower borders
Overall large flower motif

In cases where there is not a predominant motif in a pattern, or there is more than one motif, it may be necessary to search for a pattern under more than one heading.

NO GILDING

No Moulding

Blue and white
342, U177, U179, U180, U181, U182, U184, U185, U186, U187, U189, U287, U294

Monochrome Adam Buck and classical prints
1109, U65

Black and white rural prints
709, 744, 1063

Monochrome rural prints
1033, U129, U163, U283

Hand-painted rural scenes
141, U224

Black and white floral
133

Simple polychrome borders
544, U199, U300

Duvivier decorated
U3

Polychrome oriental scenes
20, 157, 421, 431, 520, 621, 1040, 1066, 1084, 1172, 1385, 3048, 3203

Monochrome bands, overdecoration
379, 382, 946, 947, U62, U79

Monochrome bands, overdecoration and floral sprays
12, 605, 662, 1180, 1363, U20, U190

Shells
1045

Baskets
171, 308, 328, 699, 746, U57

Tobacco patterns
272, U183, U301

Swags
101, 139, 415, 596, 1296, 2183, U15, U16, U17, U18, U19, U52

Pink scale borders
67, 78, 173, 273, 311, 354, 541, 686, 791, U61, U259

Simple monochrome patterns
336, 393, 401, 461, 764, 783, 798, 1623

Overall sprigs
911, 1634

Floral sprays
3, 22, 121, 140, 144, 195, 279, 296, 297, 298, 312, 353, 366, 376, 377, 442, 449, 593, 594, 603, 660, 747, 748, 749, 799, 1058, 1064, 1157, 1230, 1238, 1244, 1399, 1442, 1444, 1547, 1560, 1669, 1772, 2094, 2493, 3113, 3502, U10, U29, U55, U56, U58, U60, U63, U114, U142, U148, U257, U266

Undulating or wavy line borders
98, 122, 172, 186, 191, 208, 253, 267, 294, 295, 338, 367, 378, 420, 433, 467, 598, 599, 838, 839, 953, 1117, 1354, U39, U59, U202, U207, U241, U297

Crossing undulating or wavy line borders
241, 381, 450, U112, U216

Silver lustre
U100, U101, U102, U103, U104, U105, U106, U107, U108, U301

Bird scenes
1511, 1513, 1613, 1614, U274

Bush and tree patterns
1435, U64

Large leaf patterns
619, 928, 1070, 1618

Large flower borders
434, 1169, 1240, 1311, 1359, 1371, 1434, 1445, 1498, 1621, 1819, 1820, 1831, 2258, 2343, 2472, 3224, U125, U282, U298

Overall large flower motif
940, 1173, 1181, 1235, 2141, U206

Moulding

Bird moulding: Floral sprays
1742, 1770, 2171, 2188, 2239, 2369, U265

Flower moulding: Floral sprays
1749

Moulded flower border: Polychrome decorated flowers
U146

Moulded background: Hand-painted rural and other scenes
U131, U171, U213, U270

Moulded body: Swags
U250, U286, U296

Moulded body: Floral sprays
3035, U252

Moulded body: Primary background colour, overdecoration
U194, U226, U262

Moulding: Geometric patterns
U292

Moulded floral sprays: Blue and white
2184

Moulded floral sprays: Floral sprays
2769, 2844, 3371, U260

Basket-weave moulding: Blue and white
1929

Basket-weave moulding: Floral sprays
U136

Basket-weave moulding: Bird scenes
2383

Basket-weave moulding: Flowers in cartouches
1897, 1930, 1939, 2011, 2172, U275, U278

Basket-weave moulding: Overall large flower motif
2350

GILDING

No moulding

Blue and white
465, 473, 604, 1762, 1856, 2483, 2488, 2733, U168, U172, U175, U176, U178, U188, U191

Adam Buck and classical prints
495, 1147, 1178, U243

Polychrome Adam Buck prints
1236, 1277, 1525, U84

Black and white rural prints
462, 466, 511, 559, 1100, 475a

Monochrome rural prints
487, 874, 1507, 1725, U117, U169

Polychrome rural prints
984, 1053, 1092, 1159, 1478, 1935, 3278, U83, U116, U137, U164

Hand painted rural and other scenes
1119, 1934, 1956, U201, U267

Black and white fruit
U32

Polychrome fruit
753, 1357, U53

Black and white floral
423, U89

Black and white floral with coloured band
934, U299

Simple polychrome borders
316

Duvivier decorated
5, 11, U4, U28, U120, U277, U285

Polychrome oriental scene
425, 510, 673, 789

Monochrome bands
167, 206, 221, 222, 223, 227, 229, 231, 244, 258, 292, 2155, U66

Monochrome bands, overdecoration
124, 168, 181, 254, 257, 289, 306, 307, 313, 343, 459, 469, 472, 504, 516, 555, 558, 670, 671, 692, 695, 762, 771, 2098, 2603, U11, U35, U42, U74, U96, U229, U232

Monochrome bands, overdecoration and floral sprays
672, 676, 822, 827, 1543, 2008, 2054, 2120, 2737, U27, U73, U91, U139, U154, U227

Baskets
611

Tobacco patterns
274, 360, 490, 856, U93

Warburtons patent
840, 846, 888, 1810

Armorials
U31, U165, U284

Swags
94, 145, 152, 160, 166, 185, 209, 216, 455, 543, 545, 1059, 1152, 1428, U5, U23, U24, U33, U34, U99, U121, U217, U247, U280, U290

Mainly gold with other colours
83, 89, 199, 200, 202, 213, 259, 275, 290, 291, 300, 339, 346, 347, 348, 349, 363, 365, 369, 444, 471, 503, 568, 780, 1041, 1043, 1046, 2283, 2802, 2804, U12, U36, U86, U195, U197, U210, U211, U256, U261, U273

Simple monochrome patterns
U193

Overall sprigs
53, 161, 189, 237, 344, 546, 547, 786, 790, 2022, U291

Floral sprays
324, 373, 422, 426, 794, 1397, 1508, 1551, 1553, 1554, 1563, 1597, 1659, 1677, 2181, 2899, 2901, U109, U118, U156, U196

Primary background colour with overdecoration
565, 625, 675, 770, 777, 919, 966, 1007, 1016, 1266, 1344, 1544, 1710, 2058, 2128, 2180, 2274, 2384, 2387, 3017, 3324, U95, U97, U254, U263

Undulating or wavy line borders
84, 90, 135, 136, 196, 233, 238, 280, 288, 314, 318, 323, 350, 351, 394, 428, 430, 439, 441, 478, 480, 515, 586, 760, 775, 830, 901, 1450, U25, U47, U88, U234, U253

Crossing undulating or wavy line borders
115, 142, 148, 170, 182, 188, 266, 362, 651, U44, U81, U272

Late oriental-type scenes
570, 572, 752, 876, 1054, 1163, 1214, 1325, 1541, 2358, 2359, 3074, U152, U170, U258

Bird scenes
1681, 2102, U219

Mazarine blue
149, 150, 153, 154, 155, 156, 230, 240, 243, 248, 249, 251, 408, 411, 427, 498, 505, 527, 536, 538, 540, 551, 553, 554, 556, 563, 566, 569, 575, 581, 583, 585, 622, 623, 630, 636, 638, 644, 657, 669, 735, 736, 810, 835, 880, 882, 922, 924, 1162, 1267, 1976, U1, U2, U38, U40, U41, U67, U68, U69, U70, U71, U76, U77, U78, U80, U82, U212, U214, U231, U233, U235, U236, U238, U276, U288, U289, U295

Marble effects
647, U110

Strawberry and other fruit patterns
285, 319, 451, 533, 629, 631, 737, 738, 763, 779, 829, 1018, 1255, 1270, 1272, 1415

Bush and tree patterns
446, 484, 1373

Geometric patterns
475, 597, U119, U222

Circular devices
U54

Exotic animals
550, 761, U167

Flowers in cartouches
183, 398, 571, 653, 1057, 1398, 1857, 2275, 2881, 3050, 3829, U13, U242, U293

Scenes in cartouches
435, 436, U115, U157

Large leaf patterns
302, 329, 334, 357, 443, 443a, 521, 524, 562, 645, 781, 824, 826, 881, 1161, 1332, U87, U98, U113, U132, U147, U208

Large flower borders
317, 330, 356, 445, 499, 812, 885, 914, 921, 971, 1126, 1160, 1218, 1263, 1279, 1304, 1318, 1327, 1378, 1400, 1401, 1403, 1409, 1413, 1421, 1426, 1453, 1474, 1485, 1571, 1575, 1600, 1653, 1695, 1696, 1699, 1700, 1756, 1822, 1830, 1865, 1915, 3306, 3639, 3669, 3903, U94, U123, U128, U149, U151, U155, U158, U159, U200, U223, U237, U269

Overall large flower motif
234, 557, 678, 1085, 1153, 1219, 1221, 1313, 1361, 1411, 1458, 1496, 1542, 1641, 1680, 1978, 2179, 2576, U122, U126, U150, U209, U248

Gilding only
13, 52, 62, 64, 81, 91, 130, 138, 175, 176, 180, 198, 245, 264, 270, 271, 282, 283, 301, 303, 326, 331, 437, 542, 614, 926, 1052, 1055, 1141, 1252, 1535, 1610, 1980, 1983, 2506, U6, U7, U8, U9, U21, U30, U43, U48, U50, U51, U133, U215, U239, U245

Moulding

Bird moulding: Polychrome fruit
1706, U141

Bird moulding: Floral sprays
2825, U143, U144

Bird moulding: Large flower borders
1707, 1872, 1874, U162, U246

Moulded flower border: Polychrome rural prints
U135, U174

Moulded flower border: Shells
U160

Moulded flower border: Floral sprays
U140, U145, U271

Moulded flower border: Flowers in cartouches
1480

Moulded flower border: Large leaf patterns
U161

Moulded flower border: Large flower borders
1506, U138, U225

Moulded flower border: Overall large flower motif
1477

Moulded background: Hand-painted rural scenes
3032, U130, U221, U268

Moulding: Monochrome bands, overdecoration and floral sprays
1011, 2930, 2932, 3057

Moulded body: Primary background colour overdecorated
U173, U218, U281

Moulded body: Geometric patterns
U251

Moulded sprays: Hand-painted rural and other scenes
2229

Moulded sprays: Polychrome fruit
2240

Moulded sprays: Dr Syntax scenes
2623, 2679

INDEX 2:

List of Illustrations by Article Types

20 Ogee fluted saucer dish
23 Saucer dish; dia 21.25cm
24 Saucer dish
35 Saucer dish
55 Saucer dish; dia 19.5cm
67 Saucer dish; dia 20cm
72 Saucer dish
96 Saucer dish
103 Saucer dish
104 Saucer dish
133 Saucer dish with ring mark
136 Bone-china cockle plate; dia 11cm
140 Saucer dish
151 Saucer dish
153 Saucer dish
163 Saucer dish, New Hall 'Ring Mark'; dia 21.5cm
164 Bone-china saucer dish; dia 21.25cm
165 Bone-china saucer dish
175 Saucer dish
180 Plate
190 Saucer dish
194 Plate
196 Plate
204 Basket-weave cockle plate; dia 12.25cm
213 Basket-weave moulded plate
217 Plate
219 Plate
221 Bird-moulded plate; dia 21.5cm
225 Saucer dish
277 Saucer dish
285 Flower-moulded plate (ring mark)
310 Saucer dish
312 A 'quail' pattern plate, probably a replacement
317 Saucer dish in hard-paste porcelain
326 Plate

Bowls

6 Faceted bowl
101 Bowl
115 Bowl
118 Bone-china bowl; dia 15.5cm, height 7cm
135 Bowl with curved foot rim; dia 13cm × height 6.5cm
157 Bowl

Dessert ware

134 Dessert dish
170 Bone-china dessert dish
173 Dessert dish with bird moulding; 27.5cm × 22cm
174 Dessert plate with bird moulding
176 Sauce tureen; height 14.5cm
179 Bird moulded dessert dish
195 Basket-weave moulded dessert dish
205 Flower-moulded dessert dish with ribbon handles
206 Flower-moulded dessert dish with ribbon handles
207 Tall dessert comport; length 30cm, height 14cm
210 Basket-weave moulded dessert dish
212 Bird-moulded dessert dish; 28cm × 21.5 cm
214 Tall dessert comport with basket-weave moulding
215 Dessert plate with relief moulding
218 Relief moulded dessert dish with ribbon handle
224 Dessert dish with shell-moulded handles
226 Dessert dish with shell-moulded handles
227 Shell-moulded dessert plate
230 Bone-china dessert plate with shell moulding
272 Flower-moulded dessert dish; 19.5cm × 18.5cm
281 Dish; 31.5cm × 25cm
300 A rare shape flower-moulded sauce-tureen; height 15cm

Drinking Vessels

2 Chocolate cup and cover; height 5.25cm
3 Coffee cup with clip handle; height 6.5cm
7 Ogee fluted coffee can with ring handle
8 Reeded tea bowl with handle and saucer; height 4.75cm
14 Reeded coffee cup and saucer
15 Trio with clip handled cup
17 Saucer
22 Coffee cup and saucer; 6.5cm

263 Hard-paste coffee can
265 Cup and saucer with rare silver lustre decoration
267 Hard-paste coffee can with ring handle
268 Coffee can; height 6.25cm
269 Coffee can
270 Bute-shape cup with ring handle; height 5.75cm
273 Saucer
274 Saucer
275 London-shape coffee cup and saucer
276 Bone-china saucer
278 Bone-china cup with ring handle and saucer
279 Saucer
280 Cup and saucer (Ring Mark), Chamberlains replacement?
282 Saucer (Ring Mark), 'Haddenston Castle'
283 Saucer (Ring Mark)
288 Coffee can, plain version of patt. 570
289 Hard paste coffee can
294 Barrel-shape mug; height 8.9cm
295 A reeded and an ogee fluted coffee cup
296 Coffee cup
297 A reeded tea bowl and a plain tea bowl and saucer
298 Coffee can with ring handle
299 Coffee can with ring handle
301 Coffee can
302 Coffee can
303 A monogrammed and dated beaker
305 Coffee cup
306 London shape cup; overall height 6cm
308 Relief-moulded mug with N.H. pad-mark
315 Reeded tea bowl and saucer
319 Rare moulded tea bowl; height 5cm
320 Coffee cup; height 6.5cm (possible replacement)
321 Saucer
324 Coffee can; height 6.25cm
325 Saucer; dia 13cm

Muffin dishes
189 Muffin dish

Posset pots
42 Ogee fluted posset pot; height 9cm

Egg cups
57 Egg cup

Teapot stands
27 Ogee fluted oval teapot stand
29 Oval teapot stand
64 Oval teapot stand
234 Teapot stand
255 Silver-shape teapot stand

Coffee pots
36 Coffee pot; height 25.5cm

Sucriers
4 Round faceted sucrier; height 14cm
18 Ogee fluted sucrier
21 Oval waisted sucrier with ring handles; height 14.5cm
51 Ogee oval sucrier with ring handles and no lid
62 Tapered oval sucrier with ring handles
66 Oval sucrier with ring handles
79 Oval sucrier with ring handles; height 13.5cm
112 Sucrier; height 12.5cm
126 London-shape sucrier; height 12cm
131 London-shape sucrier; height 12cm
138 Detail from a London-shape sucrier
142 London-shape sucrier; height 12.5cm
144 Bone-china London-shape sucrier
145 London-shape sucrier
161 London-shape sucrier, 'Ring Mark'
169 London-shape sucrier
178 Fluted London-shape sucrier; height 12.5cm
185 London-shape sucrier; height 11.5cm
187 London-shape sucrier base with bracket handles
191 London-shape sucrier with bracket handles

184 London-shape creamer, high handle; height 10.5cm
197 London-shape creamer with high handle
203 London-shape creamer with high handle
208 London-shape creamer with high handle; height 11cm
264 Lustred boat-shape creamer; height 9.5cm
266 Lustred boat-shape creamer; height 9.5cm

307 An ogee fluted boat-shape creamer
313 Creamer, puce rural print (Ring Mark); height 9.5cm

Spoon trays
287 Spoon tray; 14.5cm × 9.25cm

Knives
314 Knife

INDEX 3:

Patterns Illustrated in Other Publications

422 *New Hall*, Pl. 222
425 *New Hall*, Pls 88, 223, 224
426 *New Hall*, Pl. 56, 225
427 *New Hall*, Pl. 226
430 *New Hall*, Pl. 227
431 *New Hall*, Pl. 221
433 *New Hall*, Pl. 241
434 *New Hall*, Pl. 228
436 *New Hall*, Pl. 229
437 *New Hall*, Pl. 230
439 *New Hall*, Pl. 231
441 *New Hall*, Pl. 232
442 *New Hall*, Pl. 233
445 *New Hall*, Pl. 234
446 *New Hall*, Pl. 58; *Staffs Porcelain*, Pl. 102
449 *New Hall*, Pls 38, 235
450 *New Hall*, Pl. 236
451 *New Hall*, Pl. 237
455 *New Hall*, Pl. 238
459 *New Hall and Its Imitators*, Pl. 111
461 *New Hall*, Pl. 239
462 *New Hall and Its Imitators*, Pl. 113
466 *New Hall*, Pl. 240
467 *New Hall*, Pl. 241
471 *New Hall*, Pl. 242
472 *New Hall*, Pl. 243
478 *New Hall*, Pl. 244
480 *New Hall*, Pl. 245
484 *New Hall*, Pl. 42
490 *New Hall*, Pl. N; *Staffs Porcelain*, Pl. 101
498 *British Tea Pots*, Pl. 1265
499 *New Hall*, Pl. 246
505 *New Hall*, Pl. 247
511 *New Hall*, Pl. 248
520 *New Hall*, Pl. 249
521 *New Hall*, Pl. 250
524 *New Hall*, Pl. 251
533 *New Hall*, Pl. 252
538 *New Hall*, Pl. 253
540 *New Hall*, Pl. 70
541 *New Hall*, Pl. 254
542 *New Hall*, Pl. 255
545 *New Hall*, Pl. 256
546 *New Hall*, Pl. 71
550 *New Hall*, Pl. 55
554 *New Hall*, Pl. 257
556 *New Hall*, Pl. 62
557 *New Hall*, Pl. 258
558 *New Hall*, Pl. 282

559 *New Hall*, Pl. 21
562 *New Hall*, Pl. 259
563 *New Hall*, Pl. 260
566 *New Hall*, Pl. 261
568 *New Hall*, Pl. 262
571 *New Hall*, Pl. 263
572 *New Hall*, Pl. 288
575 *New Hall*, Pl. 264
581 *New Hall*, Pl. 265
583 *New Hall*, Pl. 266
585 *New Hall*, Pl. 267
593 *New Hall*, Pl. 22
594 *New Hall*, Pl. 268
596 *New Hall*, Pl. 269
603 *New Hall*, Pl. 23
605 *New Hall*, Pl. 41
611 *New Hall*, Pl. 270; *Staffs Porcelain*, Pl. IV
621 *New Hall*, Pl. 271; *Stringer*, Pl. XXX
623 *New Hall*, Pl. 272
630 *New Hall*, Pl. 273
631 *New Hall*, Pl. 274
636 *New Hall*, Pl. 275
638 *New Hall*, Pl. 276
651 *New Hall*, Pl. 277
653 *New Hall*, Pl. 278
662 *New Hall*, Pl. 279
686 *New Hall*, Pl. 280
692 *New Hall*, Pl. 281
695 *New Hall*, Pl. 282
709 *New Hall*, Pls 44, 283; *Bicentenary Exhibit. Cat.*, p. 36
736 *New Hall*, Pl. 284
737 *New Hall*, Pl. 285
746 *New Hall*, Pl. 286
748 *New Hall*, Pl. 24; *Stringer*, Pl. XXXI
752 *New Hall*, Pls 84, 287
753 *New Hall*, Pl. 289
761 *New Hall*, Pl. 290
763 *New Hall*, Pl. 291
770 *New Hall*, Pl. 292
775 *New Hall*, Pl. 293
777 *New Hall*, Pl. 294
779 *New Hall*, Pl. 295
783 *New Hall*, Pl. 296
789 *New Hall*, Pl. 297
791 *New Hall*, Pl. 298
799 *New Hall*, Pl. 299
812 *New Hall*, Pl. 300
827 *New Hall*, Pl. 301
829 *New Hall*, Pl. 302

1897 *New Hall*, Pl. 366
1915 *New Hall*, Pl. 65
1934 *New Hall*, Pl. 367
1944 *New Hall*, Pl. 368; *Staffs Porcelain*, Pl. 104
2050 *New Hall*, Pl. 66
2082 *New Hall*, Pl. 28
2102 *New Hall*, Pl. 60
2155 *New Hall*, Pl. 369
2229 *New Hall*, Pl. 87
2240 *New Hall*, Pl. 370
2359 *New Hall*, Pl. 371
2901 *New Hall*, Pls 89, 90
3017 *New Hall*, Pl. 92
3639 *New Hall*, Pls 88, 93
U1 *New Hall*, Pl. 75
U2 *New Hall*, Pl. 76
U4 *Bicentenary Exhibit. Cat.*, p. 33
U5 *New Hall*, Pl. A; *Bicentenary Exhibit. Cat.*, p. 8
U7 *New Hall*, Pl. 16
U13 *New Hall*, Pl. 68
U24 *Bicentenary Exhibit. Cat.*, p. 16
U30 *New Hall*, Pl. 33; *British Porcelain*, Pl. 405
U43 *British Porcelain*, Pl. 406
U55 *Bicentenary Exhibit. Cat.*, p.12
U60 *Bicentenary Exhibit. Cat.*, p. 8
U67 *New Hall and Its Imitators*, Pl. 11; *Bicentenary Exhibit. Cat.*, p. 22
U100 *New Hall*, Pl. 96
U101 *New Hall and Its Imitators*, Pl. 151
U105 *New Hall*, Pl. 105
U120 *New Hall and Its Imitators*, Pl. 13

U131 *New Hall*, Pl. 48
U133 *Staffs Porcelain*, Pl. 348
U147 *Brit. Pot. & Porc.*, Pl. 444 top left; *Fine Porc. & Pottery*, p. 80
U157 *Staffs Pots & Potters*
U175 *English Blue & White*, Pl. 96D
U176 *New Hall*, Pl. 100; *Bicentenary Exhibit. Cat.*, p. 26
U178 *New Hall*, Pl. G; *Bicentenary Exhibit. Cat.*, p. 26
U179 *New Hall*, Pl. 105
U180 *New Hall*, Pl. 106
U182 *New Hall*, Pl. 107
U184 *New Hall*, Pl. 104
U185 *New Hall*, Pl. 103
U186 *New Hall*, Pl. 97; *English Blue & White*, Pl. 96A
U187 *New Hall*, Pl. 99; *English Blue & White*, Pl. 96C
U190 *New Hall*, Pl. B
U196 *New Hall*, Pl. C
U221 *New Hall*, Pl. 49
U250 *Staffs Porcelain*, Pl. 114
U259 *New Hall*, Pl. D; *Bicentenary Exhibit. Cat.*, p. 29
U260 *New Hall*, Pl. 95
U280 *Encycl. Brit. Porc. Manufacturers*, Pl. 206
U284 *English Ceramics 1580–1830*, Pl. 207
U285 *New Hall*, Pl. 114
U286 *New Hall*, Pl. 78
U287 *New Hall*, Pl. 101
U300 *New Hall and Its Imitators*, Pl. 3

Plate 1   Pattern No. 20:
High Chelsea ewer; height 7.5cm

Plate 3   Pattern No. 84:
Coffee cup with clip handle; height 6.5cm

Plate 2   Pattern No. 52:
Chocolate cup and cover; height 5.25cm

Plate 4   Pattern No. 94:
Round faceted sucrier; height 14cm

Plate 5   Pattern No. 101:
Helmet jug with clip handle

Plate 6   Pattern No. 135:
Faceted bowl

Plate 7   Pattern No. 138:
Ogee fluted coffee can with ring handle

Plate 8   Pattern No. 142:
Reeded tea bowl with handle and saucer; height 4.75cm

Plate 9   Pattern No. 145:
Faceted saucer dish

Plate 10   Pattern No. 148
Saucer dish

Plate 11   Pattern No. 149:
Ogee fluted saucer dish

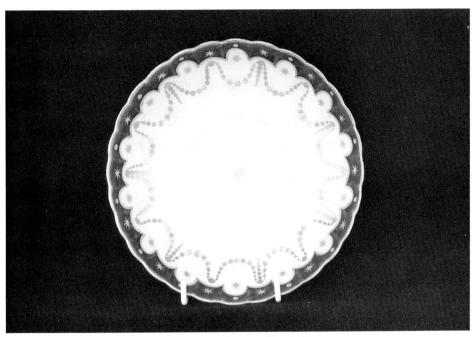

Plate 12   Pattern No. 153:
Fluted saucer dish; dia. 17.5cm

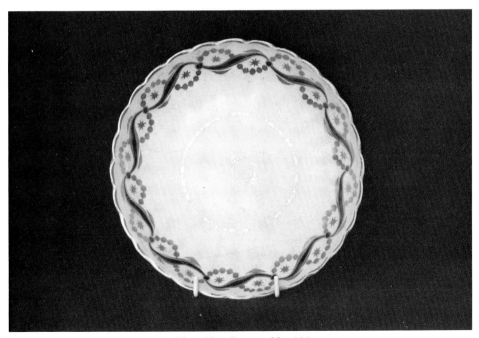

Plate 13   Pattern No. 156
Fluted saucer dish; dia. 20cm

Plate 14   Pattern No. 160:
Reeded coffee cup and saucer

Plate 15   Pattern No. 161:
Trio with clip-handled cup

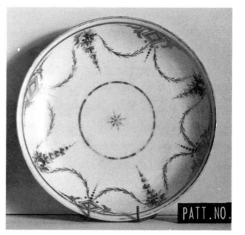

Plate 16   Pattern No. 182:
Detail of pattern on silver-shape teapot

Plate 17   Pattern No. 185:
Saucer

Plate 18   Pattern No. 189:
Ogee fluted sucrier

Plate 19   Pattern No. 195:
Ogee fluted oval jug

Plate 20   Pattern No. 199:
Ogee fluted saucer dish

Plate 21   Pattern No. 229:
Oval waisted sucrier with ring handles; height 14.5cm

Plate 22   Pattern No. 231:
Coffee cup and saucer

Plate 23   Pattern No. 233:
Saucer dish; dia. 21.25cm

Plate 24   Pattern No. 234:
Saucer dish

Plate 25   Pattern No. 238:
Oval waisted teapot; height 18cm

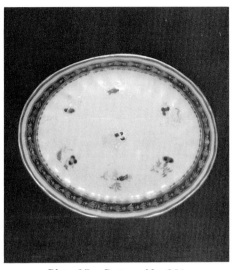

Plate 27   Pattern No. 251:
Ogee fluted oval teapot stand

Plate 26   Pattern No. 243:
Ogee fluted and waisted obconical jug;
height 12.25cm

Plate 28   Pattern No. 254:
Oval waisted teapot

Plate 29   Pattern No. 294:
Oval teapot stand

Plate 30   Pattern No. 295:
Ogee fluted boat-shape creamer; height 9.75cm

Pattern 761 Teapot: height 15.5cm

Pattern 425 Clip-handled Jug: height 19cm

Pattern 421 Coffee-pot and Stand:
height 27cm

Pattern 241 Clip-handled Jug:
height 15cm

A selection of Barrel-shaped Teapots: top left pattern 121, right pattern 20, bottom left
pattern 122, centre ref. U186, right pattern 139

A selection of Silver-shaped Teapots: top left pattern 171, right pattern 78, bottom left pattern 136, right pattern 273

A selection of Ogee-oval-shaped Teapots: top pattern 208, bottom left pattern 449, right pattern 241

A selection of Boat-shaped Teapots: top left pattern 781, right pattern 829, bottom left pattern 554, right ref. U49 marked 'Cotton High Street Edinburgh'

A selection of London-shaped Teapots: top left pattern 1614, right pattern 1695, bottom left pattern 1163, right pattern 1453

A selection of Sucriers: top left pattern 202, centre ref. U30, right pattern 319, bottom left pattern 490, centre pattern 155, right pattern 427

A selection of Sucriers: top left pattern 408, right pattern 636, bottom left pattern 306, centre pattern 213, right pattern 446

A selection of Helmet-shaped Jugs: top left pattern 89, centre pattern 140, right pattern 144, bottom left to right pattern 53, pattern 155, pattern 173, ref. U81

A selection of Jugs: top left pattern 83, centre ref. U27, right pattern 172, bottom left pattern 191, centre ref. U185, right pattern 243

A selection of Jugs: top left pattern 22, centre pattern 273, right ref. U148, bottom left pattern 222, centre pattern 296, right pattern 449

A late Sucrier of rare shape pattern 2901: height 14.5cm

A pair of well decorated dessert Plates pattern 2932: size 24.5cm

Plate 31   Pattern No. 311:
Low boat-shape creamer; height 8cm

Plate 32   Pattern No. 313:
Bute-shape cup

Plate 33   Pattern No. 329:
Silver-shape jug

Plate 34   Pattern No. 331:
Silver-shape jug

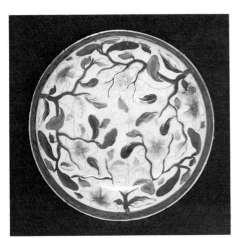

Plate 35   Pattern No. 334:
Saucer dish

Plate 36   Pattern No. 336:
Coffee pot; height 25.5cm

Plate 37   Pattern No. 343:
Coffee can

Plate 38   Pattern No. 347:
Coffee can

Plate 39   Pattern No. 349:
Tea bowl

Plate 40   Pattern No. 350:
Coffee cup

Plate 41   Pattern No. 351:
Oval jug; height 11cm

Plate 42   Pattern No. 353:
Ogee fluted posset pot; height 9cm

Plate 43   Pattern No. 356:
Silver-shape jug

Plate 44   Pattern No. 357:
Bute-shape cup and saucer; height 6cm

Plate 45   Pattern No. 378:
Saucer

Plate 46   Pattern No. 381:
Coffee cup

Plate 47   Pattern No. 393:
Silver-shape jug

Plate 48   Pattern No. 394:
Coffee cup with clip handle

Plate 49   Pattern No. 401:
Oval waisted teapot

Plate 50   Pattern No. 411:
Coffee can; height 6.25cm

Plate 51   Pattern No. 423:
Ogee oval sucrier with ring handles and no lid

Plate 52   Pattern No. 430:
Coffee can; height 6.25cm

Plate 53   Pattern No. 434:
Saucer

Plate 54   Pattern No. 436:
Bute-shape cup and saucer

Plate 55   Pattern No. 437:
Saucer dish; dia. 19.5cm

Plate 56   Pattern No. 443:
Coffee can

Plate 57   Pattern No. 446:
Egg cup

Plate 58   Pattern No. 455:
Silver-shape jug

Plate 59   Pattern No. 459:
Bute-shape cup and saucer

Plate 60   Pattern No. 462:
Boat-shape creamer

Plate 61   Pattern No. 467:
Boat-shape teapot with fleur-de-lis knop

Plate 62   Pattern No. 475:
Tapered oval sucrier with ring handles

Plate 63   Pattern No. 487:
Oval-shape teapot with a blue bat print;
height 16cm

Plate 64   Pattern No. 495:
Oval teapot stand

Plate 65   Pattern No. 510:
Low boat-shape creamer

Plate 66   Pattern No. 540:
Oval sucrier with ring handles

Plate 67   Pattern No. 545:
Saucer dish; dia. 20cm

Plate 68   Pattern No. 547:
Boat-shape creamer; height 9.5cm

Plate 69   Pattern No. 550:
Bute-shape cup; height 5.75cm

Plate 70   Pattern No. 551:
Coffee can

Plate 71   Pattern No. 556:
Coffee can

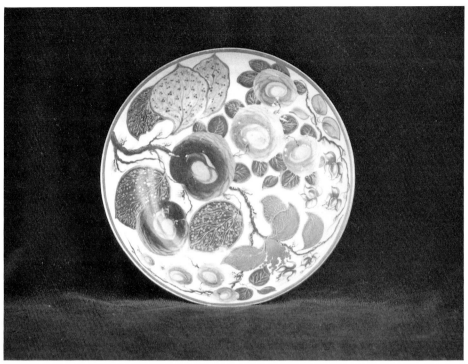

Plate 72   Pattern No. 557:
Saucer dish

Plate 73   Pattern No. 558:
Ring-handled cup and saucer

Plate 74   Pattern No. 562:
Ring-handled Bute-shape cup;
height 5.75cm

Plate 75   Pattern No. 566:
Coffee can

Plate 76   Pattern No. 568:
Ogee fluted waisted tea bowl and saucer

Plate 77   Pattern No. 569:
Oval teapot

Plate 78   Pattern No. 570:
Oval teapot

Plate 79   Pattern No. 575:
Oval sucrier with ring handles; height 13.5cm

Plate 80   Pattern No. 586:
Coffee can

Plate 81   Pattern No. 593:
Silver-shape jug; height 10.5cm

Plate 82   Pattern No. 594:
London-shape teapot

Plate 83   Pattern No. 596:
Silver-shape jug; height 10.5cm

Plate 84   Pattern No. 631:
Boat-shape teapot

Plate 85   Pattern No. 638:
Bute-shape cup and saucer

Plate 86   Pattern No. 644:
Bute-shape cup; height 5.5cm

Plate 87   Pattern No. 651:
Coffee can

Plate 88   Pattern No. 653:
Cup and saucer

Plate 89   Pattern No. 660:
Tea bowl and saucer

Plate 90   Pattern No. 662:
Small boat-shape creamer; height 8cm

Plate 91   Pattern No. 670:
Coffee can

Plate 92   Pattern No. 672:
Coffee can

Plate 93   Pattern No. 673:
Coffee can

Plate 94   Pattern No. 676:
Boat-shape creamer

Plate 95   Pattern No. 738:
Saucer

Plate 96   Pattern No. 760:
Saucer dish

Plate 97   Pattern No. 762:
Boat-shape creamer

Plate 98   Pattern No. 771:
Boat-shape creamer

Plate 99   Pattern No. 789:
Boat-shape creamer

Plate 100   Pattern No. 794:
Bute-shape cup and saucer

Plate 101   Pattern No. 798:
Bowl

Plate 102   Pattern No. 810:
Boat-shape teapot

Plate 103   Pattern No. 824:
Saucer dish

Plate 104   Pattern No. 826:
Saucer dish

Plate 105   Pattern No. 838:
Low boat-shape creamer; height 8cm

Plate 106   Pattern No. 840:
Boat-shape teapot, Warburtons Patent mark

Plate 107   Pattern No. 876:
Saucer

Plate 108   Pattern No. 882:
Coffee can with ring handle

Plate 109   Pattern No. 885:
Coffee can with ring handle

Plate 110   Pattern No. 888:
Coffee can with ring handle

Plate 111   Pattern No. 922:
Boat-shape creamer; height 9.5cm

Plate 112   Pattern No. 924:
Sucrier; height 12.5cm

Plate 113   Pattern No. 946:
Tea bowl and saucer

PATT.NO.947

Plate 114   Pattern No. 947:
Teapot; height 15.5cm (this shape paste or bone)

Plate 115   Pattern No. 971:
Bowl

Plate 116   Pattern No. 1018:
Coffee can with ring handle

Plate 117   Pattern No. 1040:
A rectangular and an oval teapot; height 15.5cm and 17.75cm

Plate 118   Pattern No. 1070:
Bone-china bowl; dia. 15.5cm, height 7cm

Plate 119   Pattern No. 1092:
Bone-china Bute-shape cup with ring handle

Plate 120   Pattern No. 1100:
Bone-china London-shape creamer; height 10cm

Plate 121   Pattern No. 1117:
London-shape teapot with ring mark

Plate 122   Pattern No. 1119:
Bone-china coffee can

Plate 123   Pattern No. 1152:
Bone-china coffee can

Plate 124   Pattern No. 1153:
London-shape creamer

Plate 125   Pattern No. 1160:
London-shape creamer

Plate 126   Pattern No. 1162:
London-shape sucrier; height 12cm

Plate 127   Pattern No. 1163:
Bone-china saucer

Plate 128   Pattern No. 1169:
London-shape creamer; height 10cm

Plate 129   Pattern No. 1173:
London-shape creamer; height 10cm

Plate 130   Pattern No. 1181:
London-shape creamer; height 10cm

Plate 131   Pattern No. 1214:
London-shape sucrier; height 12cm

Plate 132   Pattern No. 1218:
Coffee can and saucer; height 6cm

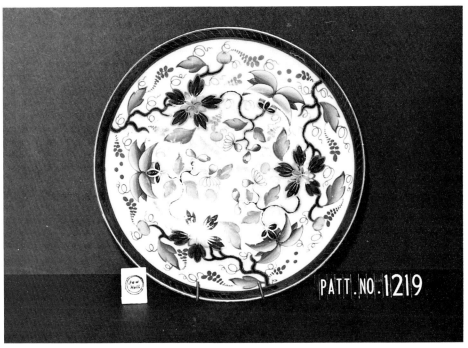

Plate 133   Pattern No. 1219:
Saucer dish with ring mark

Plate 134   Pattern No. 1230:
Dessert dish

Plate 135   Pattern No. 1244:
Bowel with curved foot rim; dia. 13cm, height 6.5cm

Plate 136   Pattern No. 1252:
Bone-china cockle plate; dia. 11cm

Plate 137   Pattern No. 1263:
Coffee can with ring handle and saucer

Plate 138   Pattern No. 1266:
Detail from a London-shape sucrier

Plate 139   Pattern No. 1277:
Cup with ring handle and saucer

Plate 140   Pattern No. 1279:
Saucer dish

Plate 141   Pattern No. 1311:
London-shape creamer

Plate 142   Pattern No. 1313:
London-shape sucrier; height 12.5cm

Plate 143   Pattern No. 1325:
Bone-china coffee can

Plate 144 Pattern No. 1327:
Bone-china London-shape sucrier

Plate 145 Pattern No. 1344:
London-shape sucrier

Plate 146   Pattern No. 1357:
Coffee can with ring handle and saucer

Plate 147   Pattern No. 1363:
Bone-china London-shape creamer

Plate 148   Pattern No. 1378:
London-shape coffee cup and saucer; height 6.75cm

Plate 149   Pattern No. 1400:
Bute-shape cup with ring handle and saucer

Plate 150   Pattern No. 1409:
London-shape creamer

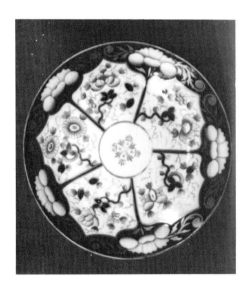

Plate 151   Pattern No. 1411:
Saucer dish

Plate 152   Pattern No. 1413:
London-shape creamer

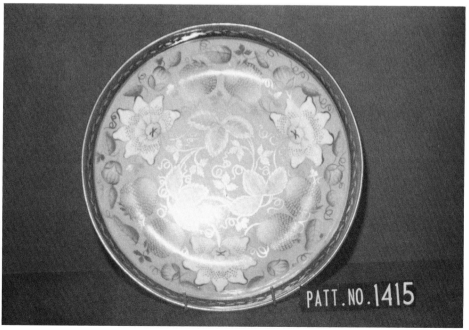

Plate 153   Pattern No. 1415:
Saucer dish

Plate 154   Pattern No. 1421:
Ring-marked London-shape tea cup and saucer; height 6cm

Plate 155   Pattern No. 1426:
London-shape cup and saucer

Plate 156   Pattern No. 1444:
London-shape creamer

Plate 157   Pattern No. 1450
Bowl

Plate 158   Pattern No. 1453:
London-shape teapot with high handle; height 15cm

Plate 159   Pattern No. 1474:
London-shape creamer, ring mark; height 9.5cm

Plate 160   Pattern No. 1508:
Cup with ring handle and saucer with ring mark

Plate 161   Pattern No. 1535:
London-shape sucrier, ring mark

Plate 162   Pattern No. 1554:
Bute-shape cup and saucer, ring mark; height 6.25cm

Plate 163   Pattern No. 1571:
Saucer dish, New Hall ring mark; dia. 21.5cm

Plate 164   Pattern No. 1575:
Bone-china saucer dish; dia. 21.25cm

Plate 165   Pattern No. 1600:
Bone-china saucer dish

Plate 166   Pattern No. 1610:
Bone-china London-shape creamer

Plate 167   Pattern No. 1618:
London-shape creamer with high handle; height 10cm

Plate 168   Pattern No. 1641:
London-shape teapot

*Plate 169   Pattern No. 1653:
London-shape sucrier*

*Plate 170   Pattern No. 1659:
Bone-china dessert dish*

*Plate 171   Pattern No. 1696:
London-shape creamer*

Plate 172   Pattern No. 1700:
London-shape creamer; height 9.5cm

Plate 173   Pattern No. 1706:
Dessert dish with bird moulding; 27.5cm × 22cm

Plate 174   Pattern No. 1707:
Dessert plate with bird moulding

Plate 175   Pattern No. 1710:
Saucer dish

Plate 176   Pattern No. 1742:
Sauce tureen; height 14.5cm

Plate 177   Pattern No. 1756:
London-shape cup and saucer

Plate 178   Pattern No. 1762:
Fluted London-shape sucrier; height 12.5cm

Plate 179   Pattern No. 1770:
Bird moulded dessert dish

Plate 180   Pattern No. 1772:

Plate

Plate 181   Pattern No. 1819:
London-shape teapot

Plate 182   Pattern No. 1820:
Round jug; height 9.5cm

Plate 183   Pattern No. 1822:
London-shape creamer, height 10cm

Plate 184   Pattern No. 1830:
London-shape creamer, high kick handle; height 10.5cm

Plate 185   Pattern No. 1857:
London-shape sucrier; height 11.5cm

Plate 186   Pattern No. 1927:
London-shape trio with Dresden-type handle

Plate 187   Pattern No. 1935:
London-shape sucrier base with bracket handles

Plate 188   Pattern No. 1939:
Saucer

Plate 189　Pattern No. 1944:
Muffin dish

Plate 191　Pattern No. 1978:
London-shape sucrier with bracket handles

Plate 190　Pattern No. 1956:
Saucer dish

Plate 192   Pattern No. 1980:
London-shape sucrier, bracket handles; height 11.5cm

Plate 193   Pattern No. 1983:
London-shape sucrier, height 11cm

Plate 195   Pattern No. 2018:
Basket-weave moulded dessert dish

Plate 194   Pattern No. 2008:

Plate

Plate 196   Pattern No. 2054:

Plate

Plate 197   Pattern No. 2094:
London-shape creamer with high handle.

Plate 198   Pattern No. 2102:
London-shape sucrier with bracket handles

Plate 199   Pattern No. 2103:
Basket-weave moulded London-shape sucrier; height 13cm

Plate 200   Pattern No. 2120:
London-shape cup and saucer

Plate 201   Pattern No. 2172:
London teapot, basket-weave moulded, high handle

Plate 202   Pattern No. 2179:
London-shape teapot with handle and no lid

Plate 203   Pattern No. 2183:
London-shape creamer with high kick handle

Plate 204   Pattern No. 2184:
Basket-weave cockle plate; dia. 12.25cm

Plate 205   Pattern No. 2226:
Flower-moulded dessert dish
with ribbon handles

Plate 206   Pattern No. 2229:
Flower-moulded dessert dish with ribbon handles

Plate 207   Pattern No. 2239:
Tall dessert comport; length 30cm, height 14cm

Plate 208   Pattern No. 2275:
London-shape creamer with high handle; height 11cm

Plate 209   Pattern No. 2283:
Cup and saucer with Dresden-type handle

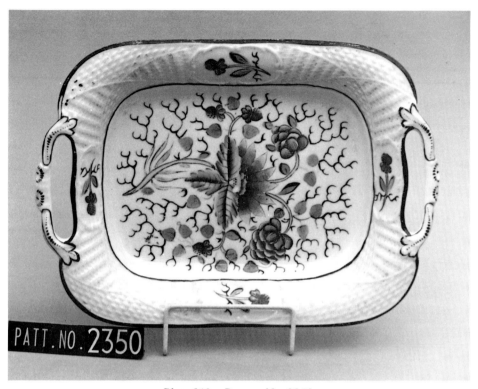

Plate 210   Pattern No. 2350:
Basket-weave moulded dessert dish

Plate 211   Pattern No. 2358:
London-shape cup and saucer

Plate 212   Pattern No. 2369:
Bird-moulded dessert dish; 28cm × 21.5cm

Plate 213   Pattern No. 2383:
Basket-weave moulded plate

Plate 214   Pattern No. 2449:
Tall dessert comport with basket-weave moulding

Plate 215   Pattern No. 2452:
Dessert plate with relief moulding

Plate 216   Pattern No. 2488:
Over-gilt London-shape cup and saucer

Plate 217   Pattern No. 2493:
Plate

Plate 218   Pattern No. 2679:
Relief-moulded dessert dish with ribbon handle

Plate 219   Pattern No. 2737:
Plate

Plate 220   Pattern No. 2804:
Cup with Dresden-type handle

Plate 221   Pattern No. 2825:
Bird-moulded plate; dia. 21.5cm

Plate 222   Pattern No. 2881:
Late bone-china cup with rare handle

Plate 223   Pattern No. 2901:
Late bone-china sucrier

Plate 224   Pattern No. 2930:
Dessert dish with shell-moulded handles

Plate 225   Pattern No. 3017:
Saucer dish

Plate 226   Pattern No. 3032:
Dessert dish with shell-moulded handles

Plate 227   Pattern No. 3035:
Shell-moulded dessert plate

Plate 228   Pattern No. 3048:
Late round teapot

Plate 229   Pattern No. 3050:
Late shape teapot (probably New Hall)

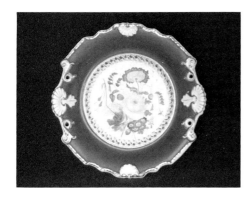

Plate 230   Pattern No. 3057:
Bone-china dessert plate with shell
moulding

Plate 231   Pattern No. 3278:
Bone-china cup with high handle and saucer

Plate 232   Pattern No. 3306:
Late bone-china sucrier (cover missing)

Plate 233   Pattern No. 3324:
Late bone-china jug

Plate 235   Pattern No. 3829:
Late shape teapot

Plate 234   Pattern No. 3669:
Teapot stand

Plate 236   Pattern No. 3903:
Late shape teapot

Plate 237   Ref. No. U3:
Saucer decorated by Duvivier

Plate 239   Ref. No. U7:
Covered cup

Plate 238   Ref. No. U5:
Early reeded tea caddy; height 16cm

Plate 240   Ref. No. U12:
Coffee cup and saucer

Plate 241   Ref. No. U20:
Clip-handled helmet jug

Plate 242   Ref. No. U23:
Tea bowl; height 5cm

Plate 243   Ref. No. U24:
Clip-handled coffee cup

Plate 244   Ref. No. U29:
Tea bowl and saucer

Plate 245   Ref. No. U36:
Saucer

Plate 246   Ref. No. U40:
Coffee cup

Plate 247   Ref. No. U61:
Helmet jug with clip handle; height 9.25cm

Plate 248   Ref. No. U62:
Tea bowl and saucer

Plate 249   Ref. No. U63:
Clip-handled coffee cup and saucer; cup height 6.25cm

Plate 250   Ref. No. U64:
Tea bowl and saucer (probable Lowestoft replacement)

Plate 251   Ref. No. U67:
Reeded coffee cup

Plate 252   Ref. No. U68:
Reeded tea bowl and saucer

Plate 253   Ref. No. U70:
Helmet jug

Plate 254   Ref. No. U78:
Reeded tea bowl and saucer

Plate 255   Ref. No. U79:
Silver-shape teapot stand

Plate 256   Ref. No. U82:
Barrel-shape teapot with clip handle

Plate 258   Ref. No. U84:
Bone-china coffee can with ring handle

Plate 257   Ref. No. U83:
Helmet-shape jug

Plate 259   Ref. No. U87:
Bute-shape cup and saucer

Plate 260   Ref. No. U94:
Coffee can with ring handle

Plate 261   Ref. No. U96:
Hard-paste Bute-shape cup and saucer, ring handle

Plate 262   Ref. No. U97:
Hard-paste coffee can

Plate 263   Ref. No. U99:
Hard-paste coffee can

Plate 264   Ref. No. U102:
Lustred boat-shape creamer; height 9.5cm

Plate 265   Ref. No. U105:
Cup and saucer with rare silver lustre decoration

Plate 266   Ref. No. U106:
Lustred boat-shape creamer; height 9.5cm

Plate 267   Ref. No. U107:
Hard-paste coffee can with ring handle

Plate 268   Ref. No. U110:
Coffee can; height 6.25cm

Plate 269   Ref. No. U113:
Coffee can

Plate 270   Ref. No. U121:
Bute-shape cup with ring handle; height 5.75cm

Plate 271   Ref. No. U133:
London-shape teapot with high handle

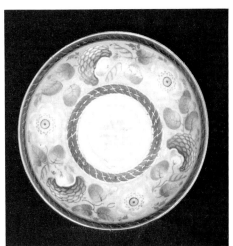

Plate 273   Ref. No. U149:
Saucer

Plate 272   Ref. No. U140:
Flower-moulded dessert dish;
19.5cm × 18.5cm

Plate 274   Ref. No. U150:
Saucer

Plate 275   Ref. No. U151:
London-shape coffee cup and saucer

Plate 276   Ref. No. U152:
Bone-china saucer

Plate 277   Ref. No. U155:
Saucer dish

Plate 278   Ref. No. U159:
Bone-china cup with ring handle and saucer

Plate 279   Ref. No. U164:
Saucer

Plate 280   Ref. No. U167:
Cup and saucer (ring mark), Chamberlains replacement

Plate 281   Ref. No. U168:
Dish; 31.5cm × 25cm

Plate 282   Ref. No. U169:
Saucer (ring mark), 'Haddenston Castle'

Plate 283   Ref. No. U170:
Saucer (ring mark)

Plate 284   Ref. No. U171:
Moulded rural scene jug, ring-marked; height 13.5cm

Plate 285   Ref. No. U174:
Flower-moulded plate (ring mark)

Plate 286   Ref. No. U175:
Tea caddy and cover; height 13cm

Plate 287   Ref. No. U176:
Spoon tray; 14.5cm × 9.25cm

Plate 289   Ref. No. U179:
Hard-paste coffee can

Plate 288   Ref. No. U177:
Coffee can, plain version of pattern 570

Plate 290   Ref. No. U180:
Three-footed jug; height 12cm

Plate 291   Ref. No. U182:
Asparagus server

Plate 292   Ref. No. U185:
Waisted oval sucrier; height 14.5cm

Plate 293   Ref. No. U188:
London-shape sucrier; height 12cm

Plate 294   Ref. No. U190:
Barrel-shape mug; height 8.9cm

Plate 295   Ref. No. U191:
A reeded and an ogee fluted coffee cup

Plate 296   Ref. No. U195:
Coffee cup

Plate 297   Ref. No. U202:
A reeded tea bowl and a plain tea bowl and saucer

Plate 298   Ref. No. U210:
Coffee can with ring handle

Plate 299   Ref. No. U211:
Coffee can with ring handle

Plate 300   Ref. No. U225:
A rare shape flower-moulded sauce-tureeen; height 15cm

Plate 301   Ref. No. U234:
Coffee can

Plate 302   Ref. No. U236:
Coffee can

Plate 303   Ref. No. U243:
A monogrammed and dated beaker

Plate 304   Ref. No. U251:
A rare shape of jug with unusual moulding

Plate 305   Ref. No. U253:
Coffee cup

Plate 306   Ref. No. U254:
London-shape cup; overall height 6cm

Plate 307   Ref. No. U256:
An ogee fluted boat-shape creamer

Plate 308   Ref. No. U260:
Relief-moulded mug with N.H. pad-mark

Plate 309   Ref. No. U247:
Rare hand-painted jug; height 14.5cm

Plate 310   Ref. No. U269:
Saucer dish

Plate 311   Ref. No. U270:
A hunting jug with rare edge moulding

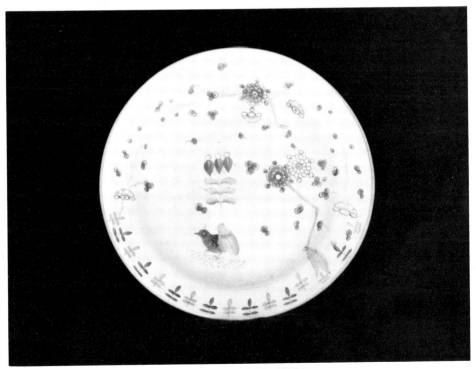

Plate 312   Ref. No. U274:
A 'quail' pattern plate, probably a replacement

Plate 313   Ref. No. U283:
Creamer, puce rural print (ring mark); height 9.5cm

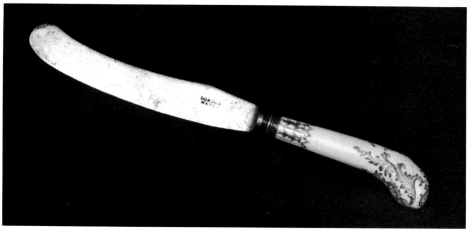

Plate 314   Ref. No. U287:
Knife

Plate 315   Ref. No. U288:
Reeded tea bowl and saucer

Plate 316   Ref. No. U289:
Silver-shape teapot

Plate 317   Ref. No. U290:
Saucer dish in hard-paste porcelain

Plate 319   Ref. No. U292:
Rare moulded tea bowl; height 5cm

Plate 318   Ref. No. U291:
Sucrier base; height 8.5cm

Plate 321   Ref. No. U294:
Saucer

Plate 320   Ref. No. U293:
Coffee cup; height 6.5cm (?replacement)

Plate 322   Ref. No. U295:
Barrel-shape teapot

Plate 323   Ref. No. U296:
Large leaf-moulded jug; height 17cm

Plate 324   Ref. No. U299:
Coffee can; height 6.25cm

Plate 325 Ref. No. U300:
Saucer; dia. 13cm

Plate 326 Ref. No. U302:
Plate